The 'Modern Writers' series

The following are titles in this new series of short guides to contemporary international writers:

Published

SYLVIA PLATH	Eileen Aird
HAROLD PINTER	W. Baker & S. E. Tabachnick
JORGE LUIS BORGES	J. M. Cohen
SOLZHENITSYN	Christopher Moody
PHILIP LARKIN	David Timms
V. S. NAIPAUL	William Walsh

In Preparation

ROBERT LOWELL   J. F. Crick

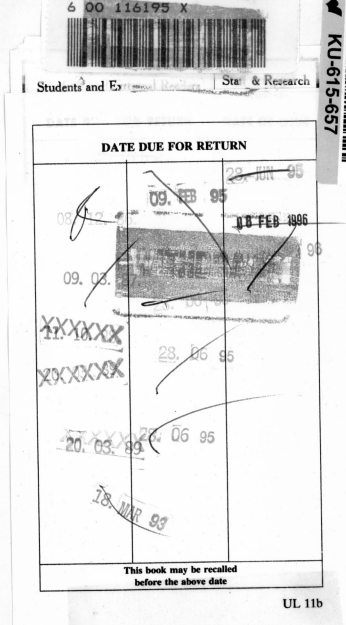

Modern Writers

Günter Grass

Irène Leonard

Oliver & Boyd
Edinburgh

Oliver & Boyd

Croythorn House
23 Ravelston Terrace
Edingurgh EH4 3TJ
(A Division of Longman Group Limited)

© Text Irène Leonard 1974

0 05 002662 3 Hardback
0 05 002661 5 Paperback

Printed in Great Britain by
Cox & Wyman Ltd
London, Fakenham and Reading

Acknowledgments

For permission to quote from the works of Günter Grass acknowledgments are due to Günter Grass and Luchterhand Verlag and to publishers of English language translations as follows: to Martin Secker & Warburg Ltd., for the British Commonwealth excluding Canada and to Harcourt Brace Jovanovich Inc., for the U.S.A. and Canada for quotations from *The Plebians Rehearse the Uprising, Cat and Mouse, Dog Years, Local Anaesthetic, Four Plays* and *Speak Out!* (all—with the exception of the excerpt from A. Leslie Willson's translation of 'The Wicked Cooks' from *Four Plays*—translated by Ralph Manheim), and for 'Stadium at Night' (translated by Michael Hamburger) and an extract from 'Diana—or the Objects' (translated by Christopher Middleton) from *Selected Poems*; to Martin Secker & Warburg Ltd., and Pantheon Books, a Division of Random House Inc., for permission to quote from *The Tin Drum* translated by Ralph Manheim (translation copyright © Pantheon Books 1961, 1962); to Martin Secker & Warburg Ltd., and MacGibbon & Kee Ltd., for 'Prevention of Cruelty to Animals' (translated by Michael Hamburger) from *Selected Poems*. Any other quotations from the works of Grass have been translated by me.

I would like to express my gratitude to Lynn Sugars who typed the manuscript, to my mother Dr. G. Heidelberger, my sister Anne Hallauer, and to other friends, notably Peter Prochnik of Royal Holloway College, London, who made invaluable suggestions on points of style. Above all, I am deeply indebted to my husband, Dick Leonard, to whom this study is dedicated.

Irène Leonard

1973

Contents

Contents

Abbreviated Titles of Günter Grass's Works Used in References

CM.	=	*Cat and Mouse*
DY.	=	*Dog Years*
GD.	=	Günter Grass: *Dokumente zur politischen Wirkung*, herausg. von Heinz Ludwig Arnold und Franz Josef Görtz, Münich 1971 (Grass Dokumente)
LA.	=	*Local Anaesthetic*
LD.	=	*Über meinen Lehrer Döblin und andere Vorträge* (On my Master Döblin and other Lectures)
P.	=	*The Plebeians Rehearse the Uprising*
Poems of G.G.	=	*Poems of Günter Grass*
Sn.	=	*Aus dem Tagebuch einer Schnecke* (From the Diary of a Snail)
SO.	=	*Speak Out!*
TD.	=	*The Tin Drum*

For further details of these works, see the Bibliography on page 111.

1 Life, Times and Literary Beginnings

Until the publication of his latest novel (*From the Diary of a Snail*), intimate details about the life of Günter Grass were hard to come by. Yet few contemporary writers can claim to have such a clearly defined public image. This discrepancy between the familiar and the unknown is no doubt deliberate. Grass's biography is not a private affair, he insists on its exemplary character, setting himself up as a prototype German of a particular generation. To a pre-election audience in 1965 he introduces himself as follows:

> Who is speaking? A story-teller. . . . And whom is he addressing? His generation. That is, the survivors of his generation. . . . Once upon a time there were thirty-eight schoolboys. All of them were born in 1922. . . . When the war was over, twelve of the thirty-eight were still alive. . . .[1]

Such extreme awareness of his own representativeness has not failed to amaze some of his colleagues and friends. Max Frisch,[2] for instance, who traces the rise of the anonymous playwright to 'Germany's Günter Grass',[3] laments Grass's refusal to leave the zone of public affairs, reproaching him gently for being immune to private problems.

That this is not so is evidenced by Grass's self-portrait—the very first of its kind—in his most recent work *From the Diary of a Snail*.[4] This portrayal is all the more remarkable as it does not shy away from revealing weaknesses as well as strengths. Those nine pages[5] are the most sensitive statement on Grass so far, welding together

1. 'The Issue' ('Es steht zur Wahl') in *SO.*, pp. 9–10.
2. Max Frisch, *Tagebuch 1966–1971*, 1972, p. 334.
3. *Time* (magazine), cover story, 13 April 1970.
4. *From the Diary of a Snail* (*Aus dem Tagebuch einer Schnecke*), 1972.
5. *Ibid.* pp. 85–94.

public and private personae. Although his self-assessment is firmly rooted in the present, reflecting moods and preoccupations of the 1960s, the past that has made Grass the vulnerable sceptic he now is permeates every one of his sentences.

His Danzig origins are a case in point. Grass's birth-place is an inexhaustible source of inspiration for all his writing, so much so that most critics claim that when he leaves his home ground, his inspiration leaves him too. Admittedly, Grass's style does change when he moves from East to West; but rather than evaluating this loss of spontaneity as one of quality, it ought to be recognised that the rootlessness resulting from the change of scenery is compensated for by greater transparency of style. To Grass, Danzig is a microcosm of Germany. This is not merely sentimental patriotism, but an opinion also held by historians. In Dr Leonhardt's book *Nazi Conquest of Danzig*, for example, we find a similar view: 'Danzig was a German microcosm. In Danzig events in the Reich were repeated in slow motion.'[6] It is primarily the Nazi period that has been the impetus behind all Grass's works.

Danzig is one of the oldest and most significant hanseatic cities on the Baltic Sea, near the mouth of the Vistula. In fact, readers of *The Tin Drum* will be familiar with its history. In the novel the various partitions of Poland and their effect on the city are evoked, not without sarcasm:

> The Peace of Oliva. How sweet and peaceful it sounds!
> There the great powers noticed for the first time that
> the land of the Poles lends itself admirably to
> partition.[7]

After having been part of Poland (1772) and Prussia (1793), Danzig was declared a Free City, quite separate from the Reich, in 1920. On 1 September 1939, just before the outbreak of World War II, it was re-integrated into the German Reich, but became Polish again in 1945. Neither German nor Polish, Danzig has always been a melting-pot of several ethnic groups with Platt, Kashubian[8] and High German as official languages. The treaty of

6. H. L. Leonhardt, *Nazi Conquest of Danzig*, 1942. p. vii.

7. *TD*. p. 389.

8. Platt is a Low German dialect; Kashubian is a Slav dialect, quite distinct from Polish.

Versailles had somewhat institutionalised this ambiguity by putting the railway and the Post Office under Polish administration. This historical ambiguity has its fictional parallel in the figures of the two Poles, Herbert Truczinski and Jan Bronski, in *The Tin Drum*, who are employed in German Danzig by the railway and Post Office respectively. In March 1945 Danzig was heavily bombed and invaded by the Russians; the large German population was forced to flee. Grass's own escape to the West has its counterpart in Oskar's flight in *The Tin Drum*.[9]

Grass's mixed parentage—his father was German and his mother Kashubian—reflects not only Danzig history, it also goes some way to explain the Polish-German tension that pervades most of his works. Thus he presents himself to an Israeli audience in 1967:

> I was born in Danzig in 1927. At fourteen I was a Hitler Youth; at sixteen a soldier, and at seventeen an American prisoner of war. These dates meant a great deal in an era that purposefully slaughtered one year's crop of young men, branded the next year's crop with guilt and spared another. You can tell by my date of birth that I was too young to have been a Nazi, but old enough to have been moulded by a system that, from 1933 to 1945, at first surprised then horrified the world. The man who is speaking to you, then, is neither a proven antifascist nor an ex-National Socialist, but rather the accidental product of a crop of young men who were either born too early or infected too late. Innocent through no merit of my own, I became part of a postwar period that was never to be a period of real peace.[10]

From 1946–8 Grass earned his living by working as a farm labourer, potash miner and stone mason. In 1949 he registered at the Düsseldorf Academy of Art, studying sculpture and painting and earning some money as a jazz drummer in the evenings. Until the mid-fifties he worked as a sculptor, graphic designer, poet and

9. *TD*. p. 413 ff.
10. 'Ben and Dieter: A Speech to the Israelis' in *SO*. pp. 89–90.

dramatist. The publication of *The Tin Drum* (1959) made him famous overnight. In the sixties he travelled extensively through America, Africa, Israel and France as well as Eastern European countries. From 1960 to 1973 he lived in Berlin with his Swiss wife, Anna, a former ballet dancer, and their four children. Günter Grass has won many prizes, including that of the Gruppe 47[11] (1958), 'Le prix du meilleur livre étranger'[12] (1961), and the Georg Büchner Prize (1965). In 1972 he was nominated for the Nobel Prize, but his compatriot Heinrich Böll received the award.

The Hitler era has marked the author to such an extent that nearly all his actions, decisions, indeed, thoughts have been profoundly influenced by this trauma. It explains, for instance, why Grass, in his self-introduction, can define himself only by negatives: 'I do not yield a picture . . . I am not consistent . . . (Absurd to reduce me to one single common denominator)'.[13] Having been deceived by Nazi glitter, it is only natural that Grass's favourite flower should now be 'light-grey scepticism, blossoming throughout the year.'[14] We understand why he can no longer 'read as absolutely'[15] as when he was fourteen, and we know what impels him to make declarations like: 'I am a Social Democrat, because socialism without democracy means nothing to me. . . .'[16]

When Grass made his literary début in 1955, such direct utterances would have been inconceivable. At that period his art did not yet show a definite political tendency. It is as a poet that Grass won his first literary recognition. He was awarded a prize in a poetry contest organised by the Süddeutscher Rundfunk in 1955. A year later Grass published and illustrated his first collection of poems, entitled *The Advantages of Moorhens*.[17] Although Grass is not a literary theorist, he has written a short essay on the nature of his poetry,[18] in which we read the categorial statement:

11. Gruppe 47 ('Group 47'), a group of authors drawn together in 1947.
12. On the publication of the French translation of *TD*.
13. *Sn.* p. 85.
14. *Sn.* p. 85.
15. *Sn.* p. 89.
16. *Sn.* p. 87.
17. *Die Vorzüge der Windhühner*, in *Gesammelte Gedichte*, 1971, pp. 19–74.
18. 'Das Gelegenheitsgedicht oder – es ist immer noch, frei nach Picasso, verboten, mit dem Piloten zu sprechen', in *Über meinen Lehrer Döblin und andere Vorträge*, (*LD*). 1968, pp. 63–6.

> Every good poem is an occasional poem. . . . He who says
> and claims this, counts himself amongst the occasional
> poets.[19]

His definition, like most of Grass's definitions, is one arrived at by
elimination: 'The occasional poet will find it difficult to supply
his method with a serious explanation'[20] in contrast to the
experimentalist, technician, 'laboratory' poet, who is able to des-
cribe his methods over many pages. Polemicising against the
conscious, often ideologically motivated poets who banish all
nouns and capital letters from their writings, Grass pleads for the
acceptance of the 'muse', even at the risk of being called old-
fashioned. When his 'muse' seeks him out, he must seize the
occasion—hence his terminology of 'occasional poetry'. The
gestation period may be long and wearisome, sometimes the
'occasion' even proves to have been a false alarm, and the
'occasional poet' has to remain silent without, however, living in
the 'proximity of the so-called unspeakable'. In short, Grass
spurns both esoteric poets and experimentalists, situating himself
somewhere in the middle.

He pleads for freedom of the imagination. In Michael
Hamburger's view:

> Grass's earlier poems eavesdrop on a primitive and
> crazy world of interchangeable functions—human,
> animal and inanimate—and seem content to leave them
> to their strange devices.[21]

These 'human, animal and inanimate functions' turn their back
on traditional poetic subjects, constituting their world from
everyday language and everyday life: ashtrays, gasmeters, bulbs,
meat, rent, kitchen windows, curtains, nuns and dolls. Objects,
animal and human situations are deliberately isolated from their
contexts and made to associate with other layers of existence,
thus establishing unknown relationships whilst exposing familiar
ones as misconceptions. The following may serve as an example:

19. *LD.* p. 63.
20. *LD.* p. 63.
21. Introduction to *Poems of Günter Grass*, 1969, p. 13.

5

'Stadium at Night'

Slowly the football rose in the sky.
Now one could see that the stands were packed.
Alone the poet stood at the goal
but the referee whistled: Off-side.[22]

The next one combines all three levels—inanimate, animate and human:

'Prevention of Cruelty to Animals'

The piano into the zoo.
Quick, get the zebra into the best room.
Be kind to it,
It comes from Bechstein.
Scores are its fodder,
and our sweet ears.[23]

Grass himself explains why he lets words and images play and interact, without forcing them into a particular view of the world

> In my poems I try ... to liberate tangible objects of all ideology, to take them apart and put them together again. ...[24]

He can liberate objects from their ideological connotations only by showing up the world in all its incongruities and contradictions. Rebelling against his experience of Fascist ideology, Grass, like other West German poets of his generation, no longer has any use for the idyllic, the tragic and the heroic. His reality can only be rendered by irony and the grotesque. His irony is not just a stylistic device, it is a principle of dissociation on the one hand, and communication on the other, establishing a new relationship

22. *Poems of G.G.*, p. 26.
23. *Poems of G.G.*, p. 26.
24. Hilde Domin (ed.), *Doppelinterpretationen*, 1966: 'In meinen Gedanken versuche ich ... fassbare Gegenstände von aller Ideologie zu befreien, sie auseinanderzunehmen, wieder zusammenzusetzen ...', p. 277.

between individual and society, spurning reconciliation and harmony if they can only be obtained at the expense of truth.[25]

The poems do not only use metaphors, they *are* metaphors. Nearly all of them are tied to objects, making sensuous experiences concrete. Not one poem represents introverted, subjective reflections; objects themselves determine the perspective, they reign autonomously. In the poem 'Diana—or the Objects' Grass actually evolves something approximating a theory of poetry. Here the huntress Diana is pointing her arrow to the artist's soul, normally an abstract concept, but Diana objectifies it:

> When she hit me,
> her object hit my soul
> which is to her like an object.[26]

Some poems, like 'The Flood' are later developed into short plays. Others like 'Open Wardrobe', 'Gasag' and 'The Eleventh Finger' prefigure motifs elaborated in *The Tin Drum*, while 'To all Gardeners' is taken up in the scarecrow ballet of *Dog Years* seven years later.

The poet Grass has been called the '"pre-form" of the epic writer'.[27] Grass himself looks at his various modes of writing as a unity, springing from one and the same form, the dialogue:

> Up to now I have written poems, plays, and prose; all
> three types of writing are, in my case, based on
> dialogue, even the poetry. And so the transition from
> poetry to drama happened like this: poems were
> written in dialogue form and were then extended. . . .
> Just like my poems and my prose, [they] contain
> fantastic and realistic elements . . . rub against each
> other and keep each other in check.[28]

25. cf. Peter Rühmkorf on Grass's poetry, in *Die Jahre die ihr kennt*, 1972, p. 106 ff.

26. From the second collection, *Gleisdreieck*, translated in *Poems of G.G.*, p. 38.

27. Lothar Baier, 'Weder ganz noch gar', in *Text und Kritik* 1a, 1970, p. 68.

28. Quoted in A. Leslie Willson, 'The Dance of Art', *Dimension* ('A Günter Grass Symposium'), 1971, p. 3.

More programmatic than his remarks on poetry is Grass's essay 'Content as Resistance'.[29] Mistrust is declared the governing principle in Grass's aesthetics. Consequently the relationship between form and content is governed by this 'mistrust', thus generating an artistic tension between truth and mediation of truth. The artist will impose a form on his content which will enable imagination and reality, fantasy and observation to coexist. Having made a case for 'occasion' as a legitimate source of creativity, Grass now proceeds to define his muse, not as the inspiring goddess of poetry, but as a 'meticulous housewife',[30] dreamless, mistrustful and grey, 'devoid of any knowledge of botany ... of the heavens, and of death—three staples of traditional content.'[31]

In 'Content as Resistance' these positions are stated in a parabolic dialogue between the esoteric, inspiration-ridden romantic Pempelfort and his antithesis, the down-to-earth and reality-bound Krudewill. A dramatisation of this conflict reaches the stage two years later in the play *Only ten Minutes to Buffalo* (1959),[32] with Krudewill as an engine driver and Pempelfort as a fireman. Mounted on a rusty old locomotive, they pretend to be driving at high speed to Buffalo. The scene of the action is a Bavarian meadow, with cows in the background. The act opens with the painter Kotschenreuther sitting in the foreground, explaining to the cowherd Axel his concept of art. Axel is bewildered by what he sees on the canvas:

> I don't get it. Every morning you come out here, you look at the cows ... and then. ... Then you make a ship out of it.[33]

To this Kotschenreuther answers portentously:

> You've got to attune yourself to the new spirit. You've got to dive down under the old values. ... Then you'll

29. 'Der Inhalt als Widerstand' in *LD*. pp. 56–63.
30. *LD*. p. 60.
31. A. Leslie Willson, *op. cit.*, p. 9.
32. *Four Plays*, 1968, pp. 165–88.
33. *Ibid*. p. 167.

> discover new aspects. . . . and first of all you've got to
> throw all these stupid titles overboard. Cow, ship. . . .
> They are all delusions. . . . Do you think your cow
> minds if you call it a sailboat . . . or even a steamer?[34]

Axel is not convinced:

> But what about my eyes? When I look and see—here a
> cow and there a ship. . . .[35]

Kotschenreuther is determined to 'open' Axel's eyes:

> That's just it, that's the big mistake. You look at things
> with your intellect. Keep your simplicity, start all over
> again from scratch. In the beginning was the ship.
> Later it developed into a cow, and the cow into a
> chess set, then the pyramids were built, then came
> journalism and with it the railroad—who knows what
> will happen tomorrow.[36]

In their own way the engine drivers exhibit the same kind of
flawless logic as the painter. Their dream of reaching Buffalo
by train is much more real to them than is the reality of the
stationary engine itself. All three, Kotschenreuther, Pempelfort
and Krudewill want to transform the world and all three fail.
Only Axel, the down-to-earth cowherd, who reappears at the end
of the play, can set the locomotive in motion. One wonders if he is
enacting the role of the grey muse, projected by Krudewill in
'Content as Resistance'.

Riding back and forth[37] is another play concerned with the theory
of drama. Its subtitle, *A Prelude on the Stage*, makes Grass's play a
parody on the prelude to Goethe's *Faust I*, which also deals with
the possibilities of the stage. As in Goethe's prelude, the cast of the
play consists of a director, a dramatist and an actor. All three
protagonists rack their brains in search of suitable forms of

34. *Ibid.* p. 168.
35. *Ibid.* p. 168.
36. *Ibid.* p. 168.
37. *Beritten hin und zurück. Ein Vorspiel auf dem Theater,* in *Akzente,* 1958, pp.
399–409.

entertainment. Nothing will do, neither sex, nor love, nor conventional plots. The most promising subject they can find is a pair of sweaty socks. The clown whom they wanted to unsaddle from his rocking-horse, sits as firmly in the saddle at the end of the performance as he does at the beginning. If there is any message to this play, it is that play writing has become an obsolete form of expression.

The Wicked Cooks[38] could also be read as a parable on the dilemma of the artist, especially as the Count, the central character of the play, was made to look like his creator, Grass, in the first production. But its value is enhanced when read as a tale on the 'human condition'. To Martin Esslin, who describes it as 'Grass's most interesting play', *The Wicked Cooks* is an 'ambitious attempt to transmute a religious subject into poetic tragicomedy.'[39] The plot is simple enough: throughout five acts a party of cooks beset an alleged Count by the name of Herbert Schymanski to disclose the recipe of an obscure grey cabbage soup to which a special kind of ash must be added. They decide to do a deal with the resisting Count. Vasco, one of the main cooks, is prepared to concede his rights to his fiancée, nurse Martha, and hand her over to the Count, provided that the latter will then divulge his secret. But when the times comes, the Count has forgotten the recipe. In the true manner of the 'occasional poet' he explains his failure to his persecutors:

> I've told all of you often enough, it is not a recipe, it's an experience, a living knowledge, continuous change— you ought to be aware that no cook has ever succeeded in cooking the same soup twice.[40]

His oppressors are closed to such subtleties. The Count elaborates:

> So I have to be more explicit. The last few months, this life with Martha. . . . It has made this experience superfluous. I have fogotten it.[41]

38. *Four Plays*, pp. 189–289.
39. Martin Esslin, *The Theatre of the Absurd*, 1968, p. 260.
40. *Four Plays*, p. 281.
41. *Ibid.* p. 281.

As the cooks relentlessly press the Count to keep his part of the bargain, the two lovers, the Count and Martha, commit suicide. Esslin substantiates his religious interpretation by pointing out that 'an analogy to the Passion pervades the play. Martha washes the Count's feet shortly before he dies, and there is an association between the mysterious food and the Eucharist, which, after all, is symbolised by a meal.'[42]

A political interpretation suggests itself just as easily. The recipe, in the Count's own words, 'is an experience, a way of life'. It cannot be handed down mechanically. The cooks may have the power but they lack sensitivity and knowledge to put it to good purpose. Herbert Schymanski, not a Count at all, is simply an aristocrat of the mind. The reverse applies to the cooks: although the white of their uniforms and the peacefulness of their trade promises innocence and bonhomie, they reveal themselves as brutes and man-hunters of the worst kind.

In *Onkel Onkel*,[43] values and preconceptions are also reversed: Bollin, a professional murderer, displays more humanity than the allegedly innocent teenagers who kill him with his own revolver. Alternatively, and this interpretation is just as viable, Bollin is evil indeed, but manages to dissemble his criminal designs so successfully, that he even arouses sympathy and compassion.

Before embarking on his murder missions, Bollin equips himself with a notebook and pencil, weapons as indispensable to him as his revolver. He is convinced that one way of possessing the world is to assail it with facts and figures, a world constituted of little schoolgirls, foresters and prima donnas. Bollin, however, is his own worst enemy, because every time, at the decisive moment, his sensitivity prevents him from committing the intended crime.

His first assignment is Sophie, a teenager lying in bed with influenza. Far from Bollin frightening her, it is Sophie's overwhelming innocence that frightens Bollin. Having been tricked by Sophie, he later takes his revenge on the doll, Pinky, by thrusting a knife into its belly. His second intended victim is the forester Greensward, who manages to divert Bollin sufficiently from his original aim by enthusing on the beauty of Baltic conifers. Bollin makes up for this failure by taking an axe and chopping a Christ-

42. Esslin, p. 261.
43. *Four Plays*, pp. 75–164.

mas tree. His third attempt is aimed at the Prima Donna Landella; in the end, Bollin runs away because he cannot bear her advances.

The last act parallels the first, giving this farce the same circular structure manifest in the others. In the prologue of the first act, the teenagers Slick and Spratt merely tease Bollin, trying in vain to obtain his watch. In the final act they go through the same sing-song ritual, confiscating one by one his watch, his pen and finally his revolver. It goes off, when playfully pointed at Bollin, who falls to the ground, dead. The revolver's determining role in this farce is a typical example in Grass's work of the autonomy of his objects; they are, as it were, acting independently.

The last play that Grass wrote in the period leading up to *The Tin Drum* is *Flood*.[44] The poem from which it arose already contains most of its elements—rain, curtains, beds, cellar, water, crates and parasols. The parasols, in both poem and play, first appear as images of adaptability and foresight, projecting a future full of sunshine. But when the flood does subside, no one is less happy about its disappearance than Yetta, the heroine:

> I wish it would rain again and rain and keep raining
> until there's water up to here. . . .[45]

The loss of excitement is harder to bear than was the ordeal they had to endure during the flood.

Grass's surrealistic imagination, playfulness, not to say tomfoolery, in his work written before *The Tin Drum* may not be essential to his literary personality. Yet many of his early metaphors prefigure later ones in the novels. They are unifying elements in his work. It is true, therefore, that Grass's early poetry and plays lay the foundation of his curious universe of nuns, nurses, cooks, dogs, scarecrows and—tin drums.

44. *Ibid.* pp. 1–74.
45. *Ibid.* p. 74.

2　*The Tin Drum*

Grass's dramatic productions made little impact on the stage; a failure that proves to have been a blessing in disguise, for the author claims

> ... *The Tin Drum* would never have been written if the West German theatres had treated me a little more kindly.[1]

Even before its publication in 1959, *The Tin Drum* was acclaimed by the Gruppe 47, which bestowed its annual prize, then one of the most prestigious literary awards in Germany, on the novel (1958). The book disoriented critics and readers alike, for their obituaries on the novel as an art form were suddenly shown to be premature. Described by a leading German critic as 'this explosion of pent-up epic energy',[2] *The Tin Drum* was universally hailed as a masterpiece.

This consensus on the aesthetic value of the work did not, however, extend to its moral assessment. Some critics[3] condemned it as a brilliant exercise in blasphemy and pornography, others[4] welcomed it as a sensitive exploration into the rise and fall of the Third Reich. The latter appraisal, although more valid, is also potentially misleading, for *The Tin Drum* is not a heavy-handed

---

1. Quoted and translated from W. J. Schwarz, *Der Erzähler Günter Grass*, 1969, p. 85: '*Die Blechtrommel* wäre wahrscheinlich nie geschrieben worden, hätten mich die westdeutschen Theater ... etwas freundlicher behandelt' (from an interview with R. Kirn in *Frankfurter Neue Presse*, 14.11.1959).

2. Marcel Reich-Ranicki, 'Unser grimmiger Idylliker' in *Deutsche Literatur in West and Ost*, 1963.

3. E.g. Günter Blöcker, 'Zurück zur Nabelschnur' in G. Loschütz, *Von Buch zu Buch*, 1968.

4. E.g. Karl Migner, 'Der getrommelte Protest gegen unsere Welt. Anmerkungen zu Günter Grass Roman *Die Blechtrommel*', *Welt und Wort*, **15** (1960).

reckoning with the German past. On the contrary, it abounds in such original humour that one might well be oblivious to the urgency of its subject matter, if it were not for the patterns underlying the novel, which reveal a deeply-felt concern.

The Tin Drum can be read on two levels, one realistic, the other symbolic. Ostensibly, it is the life-story of the dwarf Oskar, who recounts his exploits in the pre-war, war-time and post-war periods. From his bed in a mental institution, Oskar introduces us to his Kashubian grandmother Anna Koljaiczek and her four skirts that served not only as a hideway for his fleeing grandfather, but also remained Oskar's favourite place of refuge. Out of the union between Joseph Koljaiczek and Anna was born Agnes, Oskar's mother. Although Agnes was legally married to the grocer Matzerath, there is another man in her life, Jan Bronski, who, in Oskar's view, is more likely than Matzerath to be his father.

Oskar is born 'as one of those clairaudient infants whose mental development is completed at birth.'[5] He would rather not have been born at all, but the 'prospect of the drum . . . prevented [him] . . . from expressing . . . [his] desire to return to the womb'[6] At the age of three he puts into practice a long-cherished plan, stops growing and becomes a drummer. His mother, in contrast to his putative father Matzerath, sympathises with his drumming ambitions.

To defend his drum from trespassers—and there are many— Oskar develops another skill; he learns how to shatter glass with his voice. Although, initially, he only 'mobilises his vocal chords' for the purpose of protection, later on he sings 'out of pure playfulness, becoming as it were, a devotee of art for art's sake'.[7] About his drum he says 'I never played, I worked on my drum',[8] a distinction to which he clings throughout. His drumming 'work' takes him to political meetings, and even leads him into drumming contests with Jesus.

With the rise of National Socialism, Oskar finds himself more and more isolated. His mother dies, so does his friend Herbert,

5. *TD*. p. 42.
6. *TD*. p. 44.
7. *TD*. p. 68.
8. *TD*. p. 60.

and the Jewish toy merchant Markus commits suicide on the Crystal Night.[9] Oskar laments his plight in his 'rather arbitary interpretation of the Corinthian letter', a chapter that constitutes both the nucleus and the climax of the novel.

Left with his drum as his only comfort and *raison d'être*, he concentrates more and more intently on it, even though the political climate is against him and replacements become increasingly difficult to find as the Nazi threat grows. Driven by the need to repair his drum, Oskar makes his way to the Polish Post Office, and fortuitously becomes involved in its defence at the time of the German invasion of Poland in September 1939.

After Jan Bronski's execution, Oskar is left entirely to his own devices. Maria, his first love, compensates for much of his emotional disarray, until she, too, is snatched away from him by his presumptive father Matzerath. She gives birth to a son, Kurt, who, Oskar swears, is his own child. Oskar then decides to join Bebra's theatre, a touring company of dwarfs providing entertainment for German soldiers; but he is determined to return from the front for his son's third birthday in order to present him with a drum; for Oskar's dream is to establish a 'dynasty of drummers'. Kurt, however, has different ideas. Retrospectively, Oskar rationalises that his son's rejection of himself is, after all, analogous to his own rejection of Matzerath

> as though it were not just as nauseating for a young
> hopeful to take over a tin drum as to step into a
> ready-made grocery store.[10]

Matzerath's death marks the next decisive stage in Oskar's life. His father's funeral coincides with the German capitulation. At the cemetery, Oskar decides to externalize his coming of age by resuming growth and burying his drum. In Düsseldorf, where the family has moved, a drumless Oskar contributes to their upkeep, first as a stone mason's apprentice, then as an artist's model. But

9. Crystal Night. A pogrom organised by the National Socialists against German Jews on the night of 9 November 1938, so called because of the breaking of windows of a large number of shops and other buildings owned by Jews.
10. *TD.* p. 341.

attempts 'to become a good citizen'[11] are thwarted by the widowed Maria's refusal to marry him.

After a long period of deprivation, he returns to his drum, this time as a highly successful professional jazz drummer. He becomes a celebrity, but loneliness and fear of life haunt him more relentlessly than ever. He has himself locked up in a mental asylum by fabricating a criminal charge in which he is the culprit. Unfortunately for him, he is acquitted at the end of the novel. At the age of thirty, he faces his discharge into a hostile world where the Black Witch, the omnipresent personification of his own insecurity, threatens his existence.

This summary of the plot scarcely hints at the symbolism which underlies the narrative. The first question arising on a symbolic level concerns Oskar's stature. Why is Oskar a dwarf? Why a crippled dwarf? Oskar himself informs us that he decided to interrupt his growth in order to keep adults at a distance. As a precocious infant he has already seen through the moral bankruptcy of his parents, so that his stature represents a deliberate act of protest, an act based on a refusal to adapt to his surroundings, even physically. In the pre-war years, up to the German capitulation, Oskar's gnome-like appearance is to be considered as an asset: whilst the adults blindly prepare their own destruction, Oskar is retreating behind the guise of a three-year old, offering—within his limitations—some measure of resistance to National Socialism.

After the German capitulation, the demands made on him are of a different order. During the Nazi period Oskar's withdrawal into infancy was the only way to play the part of the critical observer, and yet survive; after 1945, the time had come for him to leave his hideaway and to participate openly in the reconstruction of West Germany. Oskar recognises this necessity and decides, however reluctantly, to sacrifice the advantages of childhood by resuming growth. He is only partly successful: his height increases, but he develops a hunchback.

His symbolic role has changed. During the war Oskar's diminutive size may have been a defect in the eyes of the Nazis, but the reader knows that he represents a sane element in a crippled society. After the war, disguises have become super-

11. *TD.* p. 452.

fluous, and Oskar's resumed growth possibly symbolises Germany's coming of age. Oskar's diseased back, on the other hand, may signal the resurgence of tendencies opposed to a genuine German liberation. Grass implies that the affluent society is a mere façade. In reality, a promising post-war Germany has developed into a hunchbacked cripple. However, the author of *The Tin Drum* does not leave his reader on such a pessimistic note. It is true that the hunchbacked Oskar represents the Germany of the 'economic miracle' of the 1950s, because, in contrast to his deliberately interrupted growth at the beginning, his hunchback is anything but self-willed. Yet, the author intimates that the disease might possibly be cured. He conveys his hopes only metaphorically. We are still very far away from the clearly formulated postulates we meet in his later work. The main symbol of the novel is the drum. Although so far we have dealt only with the drummer, it is the drum that leads us into the centre of the work. The very title has already told us so; as Heinz Ide points out,[12] the novel is called *The Tin Drum* and not *The Tin Drummer*.

The instrument is Oskar's medium for art, but also for protest. Artist and protester converge in the drum, or, to put it differently, Oskar's art itself is protest. Furthermore, Grass does not choose a proper drum, but one made of tin, a cheap toy for children. The tinny sound of Oskar's protest in no way reflects on its quality; it does, however, shed some light on its efficacy. Whatever the strength of Oskar's impulse, the resonance of his drumming is so weak, that in the end it can only bear witness to his helplessness. Oskar is the first to realise the fragility of his protest. How can his improvised rhythms successfully resist the organised brutality of the SA men? Here he comments on the SA sacking of Markus's shop:

> They didn't like my drum. My own drum couldn't stand up to their rage; there was nothing it could do but bow down and keep quiet.[13]

The drum symbol is anticipated in the red and white painted

12. 'Dialektisches Denken im Werk von Günter Grass', *Studium Generale* **21**, 1968, pp. 608–22.

13. *TD*. p. 197.

fence of the Polish Patriot and fire-raiser, Koljaiczek. The equally fiery red and white tongues painted on Oskar's drum can accordingly be interpreted as colours of protest. The above-mentioned distinction made by Oskar between his drumming and his glass-shattering, as one between work and play, is also an unequivocal indication of the moral purpose of his art. The drumming is creative, either as art or as protest, while his glass-shattering, playful and arbitrary, is destructive. Another image is the 'moth between the light-bulbs that drummed in the hour of his birth.' If one takes light to stand for knowledge and truth, Oskar's art of drumming means also the search for, and the dissemination of truth.

Such fundamental images justify an interpretation of the drum as an instrument of protest. This protest, which is initially an undifferentiated rejection of the adult world, is more clearly defined in the course of the novel. It is directed against three aspects of life, or, in biblical terms, it is aimed at the deliberate misinterpretation, indeed contempt, of the three theological virtues referred to in the thirteenth chapter of the first letter to the Corinthians: Faith, Hope and Love.

Oskar's protest is most conspicuous in the realm of politics, a secularised version of hope. Although far from being a heroic resistance fighter, the gnome does his best to embarrass the Nazis. In the chapter entitled 'The Rostrum', Oskar succeeds through his drumming in transforming a Nazi gathering into an orgy of wild dancing. After the event, he tries to disclaim any credit for it. He objects strongly to being hailed as a resistance fighter, warning the reader that the term has become dangerously fashionable. His actions were not politically motivated, but based on purely private dislikes, and, to confuse the reader completely, he explains how he employed the same tactics at Communist and Catholic reunions.

In fact, Oskar's elaborate refutation of involvement becomes a proof of the depth of his rebellion. For we know from the whole of Grass's work—and *The Tin Drum* is no exception—that *all* types of dogmatic thinking are suspect to him, whether he is dealing with Catholicism, National Socialism or Communism. He finds all 'isms' equally objectionable, for where blind faith replaces doubt, man abdicates his responsibility. If Oskar succeeds in puzzling all the organisations that base their creed on dogma, he places himself in the service of critical reason, and therefore performs a valuable task, whether he knows it or not.

The other major episode where the drum functions clearly as an instrument of political morality, is 'The Polish Post Office'. The Nazis have invaded Danzig, and Oskar is once more disturbed by the state of his 'mortally wounded drum'. He himself establishes a link between the dying drum and the Nazi brutality tracing back to 9 November 1938 (the Crystal Night) as 'the exact date when [his] complex was born . . . for that was the day, when [he] lost Sigismund Markus, who had kept [him] supplied with drums.'[14] It is true that the Nazis manage to capture the Polish Post Office, but at the same time, Oskar becomes the recipient of a new drum. This result makes him conclude 'Oskar had managed to save a new instrument . . . so lending some significance to the defence of said Post Office.'[15] Thus the unsuccessful defence of the Polish Post Office is transformed into a battle for Oskar's drum, and its final conquest amounts to a moral victory.

Oskar's protest, as has already been suggested, is not solely confined to an attack on dogmatic thinking in the political field, he objects just as violently to the dangers of blindly accepted religious beliefs. Already the introduction to his attitude to the Church is worth noting—'without my drum I should never have touched my forehead, chest and shoulders, making the Catholic cross.'[16]

Only criticism can save him from the fascination that Catholicism holds for him. On the other hand, he feels that the Church above all other places ought to be the rightful home for his drum, for both drum and Church have pledged themselves to fight for the highest ideals of mankind, for Faith, Hope and Love.

When he finds himself face to face with the statue of young Jesus, he is thunderstruck by his physical resemblance to it:

> I take a good look at Jesus and recognise my spit and image. He might have been my twin brother. He had my stature and exactly my watering can. . . . He looked

14. *TD*. p. 204.
15. *TD*. p. 252.
16. *TD*. p. 131.

out into the world with my cobalt blue Bronski eyes
and—this was what I resented most—he had my very
own gestures.
My double raised both arms and clenched his fists in
such a way that one wanted desperately to thrust
something into them, my drumsticks for example. If
the sculptor had done that and put a red and white
plaster on his pink little thighs, it would have been I,
Oskar's very own self, who sat there on the Virgin's
knee, drumming the congregation together.[17]

Oskar tries to make his 'double' drum, drum in Oskar's sense,
that is, protest against inhumanity. What he wants is a 'little
private miracle',

something that would make it clear to him once and
for all whether he should drum for or against; all he
wanted was a sign to tell him which of the two blue-
eyed identical twins was entitled and would be entitled
in future to call himself Jesus.[18]

But, by not drumming, Jesus fails him, and Oskar deduces from
this disappointment that the role of the protestor is reserved for
him alone. God may still exist, but His Son's refusal to drum
confirms his powerlessness in the face of war and persecution.[19]
The outcome of this experiment strengthens his resolve 'to keep on
drumming and drumming', while 'Jesus will go down into the
grave', and Oskar is convinced that 'he is a realer Jesus' than
Jesus himself.[20]

After the war, Oskar puts Jesus to the test yet again, this time,
however, only to see Jesus's previous failure confirmed. But when
the statue does drum, against all his expectations, Oskar is even
more enraged. To drum *after* the war is not only pointless, it is
treacherous. Such a misappropriation only debases the act of
drumming. Besides himself with fury, Oskar commands Jesus:

17. *TD*. p. 136.
18. *TD*. p. 138.
19. Karl Migner, *op. cit.*
20. *TD*. p. 138.

Give me back my drum this minute. You've got your cross, that should do you.[21]

Whereas Jesus' cross has proved a fraud, Oskar's drum still has all the makings of an authentic cross in the secular sphere, and if Jesus frivolously abuses the drum, he invalidates its integrity as a symbol of protest. Oskar takes leave of Mother Church and Jesus by hurling a final declaration of hatred at the Saviour:

You bastard, I hate you, you and all your hocus-pocus.[22]

The third and final sphere in which Oskar protests is the realm of love, where the drum plays as full a part as in politics and religion. The purest form of love as taught in the New Testament is compassion for the suffering. In Oskar's case, this love expresses itself most vividly in his relationship to Markus, the Jewish toy merchant and source of his drums. A close link is therefore established between Oskar, the protester against National Socialism, and Markus, its victim.

Not only does Oskar take pity on Markus when the SA man Meyn evicts him from the cemetery at Agnes's funeral, not only does he run away from Matzerath during the Crystal Night to warn Markus, while his presumptive father 'took advantage of the opportunity to warm his fingers and his feelings over the public blaze,'[23] but Oskar actually calls Markus the keeper of his drums'[24] and calls himself 'possibly his drummer'.

The Jewish survivor Fajngold, too, belongs to the realm of love. In the same way that Markus looks after Oskar's spiritual welfare, Fajngold takes care of Oskar's physical health. He disinfects him and he is also the one who stops the merry-go-round in Oskar's feverish nightmare.[25] Neither of the two Jews are particularly admirable as such; they only appear as helpless victims, but the important thing to remember is the interrelation between the

21. *TD.* p. 351.
22. *TD.* p. 351.
23. *TD.* p. 196.
24. *TD.* p. 161.
25. *TD.* p. 405.

sufferers and the drum. The characters' attitude to the drum reveals their political and moral tendencies. For instance, it is hardly accidental that Matzerath is Oskar's most half-hearted drum supporter. He is an opportunist in politics, he 'always had to wave, when other people were waving,'[26] as well as in his private life. One need only recall the unfeeling seduction scene between him and Maria, which Oskar gracelessly interrupts by jumping on Matzerath's back. He expresses his indignation by 'drumming' his version of love to contrast it with his father's selfish act of gratification:

> Then [Matzerath] bit into the velvet cushion again and [Maria] screamed: go away, and he wanted to go away, but he couldn't because Oskar was on top of them before he could go away, because I had plunked down my drum on the small of his back and was pounding it with the sticks . . . because my drum was louder than their go away, because I wouldn't allow him to go away as Jan Bronski had always gone away from my mother. . . . But I couldn't bear to see it.[27]

The three main themes of politics, religion and love merge in the above-mentioned chapter 'Faith, Hope, Love'. Here, as elsewhere, it is the drum which holds them together. Oskar's protest against the perversion of these three absolutes into their opposites is in his own words a subject that 'calls for an orchestra of ravenous wild men'.[28] Faith in the Saviour turns out to be faith in the 'gasman' Hitler, altruistic love is practised as the most ruthless form of egotism, and hope, 'man's chance of bringing social order out of chaos'[29] has become a meaningless yearning for an unspecified end.

'When a whole society fails, Oskar finds his responsibility. His deep and acknowledged involvement is reflected in the style of

26. *TD.* p. 147.
27. *TD.* p. 280.
28. *TD.* p. 191.
29. Ann Woods, 'A study of *Die Blechtrommel* by Günter Grass', M.A. thesis, (Liverpool), 1966.

the chapter.'[30] Oskar's detached fairy-tale manner makes room for intense compassion whenever he abandons the third person for the first. This applies to all the paragraphs dealing with Markus, especially towards the end, where he unequivocally conjures up the solidarity between drum, drummer and keeper of drums:

> As for me, they took away my toy merchant, wishing with him to banish all toys from the world.[31]

Markus, Oskar and the drum all stand for the fight against injustice and brutality, against the dictatorship of the 'heavenly gasman'. The fact that Markus is the source of Oskar's instruments stresses the moral content of his drumming; on the other hand, Markus's suicide betrays the precariousness of Oskar's protest.

As the drum is so central to the work, its absence must be just as significant. Since its burial coincides with that of Matzerath who had choked to death by trying to swallow the party badge, an analogy between Matzerath's funeral and the funeral of Nazi Germany suggests itself. Faced with a changed historical situation, Oskar has to adjust to a potentially new German society. Whereas during the Hitler regime he used his art as a legitimate form of secondary action, the transformed situation of 1945 calls for more direct activity.

After a heart-searching self-interrogation of 'should I or shouldn't I?' bury my drum, Oskar's 'problem was simplified, transformed into a demonstrated, wreathed, aimed and triumphant "I should"'[32] which is subsequently rephrased as: 'it must be'. Oskar will try to become a useful member of society without the intermediary of art. He develops unfamiliar feelings of responsibility, and, when Maria expresses concern about the household leaning too much on his financial support, he assures her 'that he likes nothing better than to bear a heavy responsibility'.[33]

His efforts to educate himself, and his proposal of marriage to

30. *Ibid.*
31. *TD*. p. 200.
32. *TD*. p. 396.
33. *TD*. p. 452.

B

Maria which she declines, are part of his move towards integration. Dogged by a sense of failure, Oskar finds growing a more painful process than its interruption has ever been. He quits stone masonry, leaves the family home and is eventually driven back into the position of an outsider; 'Oskar remembered his hump and fell a victim to art'.[34] Art at this stage means being a model at the Düsseldorf Academy. When one of the students, Raskolnikoff, tempts him to become an active artist again and resume drumming, Oskar resists until shortly after Maria's refusal to marry him, a rebuff exacerbated by his equally unrequited love for the nurse Dorothea.

More portentous than these psychological speculations are the political implications of Oskar's return to his drum. As the post-war 'binge' had only been a 'binge', as defeated Germany deteriorated more and more into a 'bourgeois smug' society, eager to bury its past without drawing the necessary lessons from it, Oskar had to resume his protest.

Many critics interpret Oskar's return to the drum as a return to irresponsibility. Idris Parry, for instance, explains its resuscitation in this light, because to him, contrary to our own interpretation, Oskar's drum is 'the source and symbol of his antisocial nature'.[35] This is the reason why the drumming and drumless Oskar are usually considered as two different *personae*. Oskar, however, explicitly warns the reader against such a one-sided interpretation:

> Here I could embark on an essay about lost innocence, a comparison between two Oskars, the permanent three-year-old drummer and the voiceless, tearless, drumless hunchback. But that would be an over-simplification and would not do justice to the facts.[36]

Although we have every reason to distrust Oskar's running commentary on his life, his acts prove him right in this instance. Far from observing a break in his character, we witness his

34. *TD*. p. 453.
35. I. Parry. 'Aspects of Günter Grass's narrative technique', *Forum for Modern Language Studies*, **3**, 1967, pp. 99–114.
36. *TD*. p. 490.

continual progression in ethical awareness. Even when he takes up drumming again, Oskar continues to support Maria. He speaks up for the nun raped by Lankes and accuses the latter of inhuman behaviour. The episode at the end of the novel, in which he saves Victor Weluhn from his persecutors[37] crowns his conscious defence of humanity; here, too, the drum plays a considerable part.

Heinz Ide sums up Oskar's moral evolution from intuition to awareness when he writes:

> Oskar arrives at that level of reflective consciousness,
> which his grandmother lives out intuitively.[38]

When Anna Bronski protects the fugitive Koljaiczek from his persecutors, she returns a responsive echo to the needs of the world. Oskar begins like his grandmother, but when he stands up for Victor Weluhn, this intuitive response has spiralled into a conscious one, whose source is comprehension. We have come full circle, in the sense that the drum is a circle. But Oskar's drum has shown itself to have depth as well as surface.

37. *TD*. pp. 564-5.
38. *TD*. p. 615

3   *Cat and Mouse*

After the eruption of *The Tin Drum*, the discipline of its successor, *Katz und Maus* (1961),[1] comes as a surprise. This novella is both a concentrate and a continuation of its predecessor. It fictionalises the same milieu as *The Tin Drum*, but, unlike the novel, it restricts itself to the war period. Both accounts are presented as biographies of their respective heroes, with the major difference that Oskar is himself the author of his life story, while Mahlke's account is related to us by his friend and foe, Pilenz.

Mahlke, the central character of *Cat and Mouse* is neither a 'clairaudient infant', nor a hunchbacked dwarf, nor an inmate of a mental asylum. Although he himself is sane, the world in which he lives and the times which encircle his life-span are anything but sane. In contrast to Oskar's life, Mahlke's unfolds during the war years only, the pre-war and post-war eras are only faintly sketched in by his chronicler Pilenz. Mahlke, like Oskar, is essentially a loner, only his physical abnormality does not consist of stunted growth but of an outsized Adam's apple. It is not until his persecutors exploit his physical defect, however, by placing a cat on Mahlke's Adam's apple which the animal takes for a mouse, that Mahlke is made aware of his physical defect, an awareness that escalates into an all-consuming passion.

Thus Mahlke's life is centred on one *idée fixe*: how to find an adequate compensation for, or as his narrator terms it, counter-weight to his Adam's apple. He tries screw drivers, tin openers, pompoms, neckties—nothing will do the trick. His 'distinguishing mark',[2] his 'piece of cartilage',[3] his 'elevator', his over-developed fruit' 'was large, always in motion, and threw a shadow'.[4] The

1. *Cat and Mouse*, 1971.
2. *CM*. p. 71.
3. *CM*. p. 9.
4. *CM*. p. 5.

26

eternal cat would not let itself be distracted from the eternal mouse because Mahlke's mouse 'was insatiable'.

Until one day, a gloriously decorated lieutenant makes a speech at Mahlke's school, exhibiting the Knight's cross on his neck. This experience turns into a revelation: Mahlke has discovered the one and only feat that would bring about appeasement, in his case, recognition, acclaim, admiration. During the speech Mahlke bares his neck for the first time, throwing his pompoms under the bench. At long last he has found the only effective medicine to his destructive inferiority complex. His new ambition to reach for the highest military honour that the National Socialist regime can offer, makes his schoolboy swimming and diving achievements look pale in comparison. By the time a second lieutenant, also complete with a Knight's cross, makes his entry into the Conradinum Gymnasium, Mahlke decides to steal the medal in order to rehearse its effect on him—'For the first time the Adam's apple . . . had found its exact counterweight.'[5]

But, being an honest boy, he returns the medal to Klohse, the principal of the school, who defends the 'Conradinum spirit' by throwing him out. In spite of previous reservations, Mahlke now volunteers for the army and, within a very short time, is awarded the Knight's cross himself. His last remaining ambition is to impress his new status on his old school—without this finale all his glory would be to no avail. But Klohse bars him from the auditorium, because of his past 'scandalous behaviour'. This refusal breaks Mahlke, he becomes a deserter and finally commits suicide (or so one assumes) by seeking refuge in the wrecked minesweeper *Rybitwa*, battleground for all his schoolboy feats, the scene of his apprenticeship for later 'bravery'.

Like *The Tin Drum, Cat and Mouse* exists on two levels: the universal and the political. It is the universal level that makes this novella a continuation of *The Tin Drum*. Fundamentally, there is the same pattern in the first three novels: Mahlke's cat is the archetypal persecutor; it corresponds to the Black Witch in *The Tin Drum* and to the dogs in *Dog Years*. In all three cases the symbol stands for the destructive elements in society in general and for National Socialism in particular. All three symbols are immediately recognisable by the threatening colour of black. The

5. *CM.* p. 80.

27

cat also has its human counterparts: in *The Tin Drum* it was just the shadowy figure of Luzi Rennwand,[6] in *Cat and Mouse*, nearly all the characters exhibit a cat mentality, particularly Pilenz and Klohse, who are the main culprits in bringing about Mahlke's downfall.

Apart from the fundamental link between persecutor and persecuted, there is the response of the persecuted to his situation that creates the affinity between Mahlke and Oskar. Grass's protagonists develop external and internal defence mechanisms to protect themselves from their persecutors. The external ones consist of seeking out places of refuge, where they are cut off from the world and as close to a state of oblivion as possible. Oskar would dearly have loved to creep back to his mother's womb, instead of which he has to make do with the second-best offer of his grandmother's skirts, of which his hospital bed is only a modern version.

Mahlke's flight from the hostility of his surroundings takes him to the bowels of the Polish minesweeper, *Rybitwa*. However, his refuge, unlike Oskar's is not a refuge in the full sense of the word, because the *Rybitwa* is not only a hiding place, but also a hunting ground. Thus, unlike Oskar, Mahlke transfers his conflict to the ship, instead of escaping from it. Mahlke's retreat from the world is at the same time a desperate rush towards it. Only at the end does the minesweeper return to its original function, this time as a place of eternal refuge.

In *The Tin Drum*, Oskar's external defences have their internal counterpart in his refusal to grow, a gesture symbolising outright rejection of society. But Oskar adapts his decision to changing circumstances, for, after the German capitulation, he considers a future within society and resumes growth. We leave Oskar preparing himself for a confrontation with the Black Witch. Mahlke acts, as it were, on Oskar's rational insight that a *modus vivendi* with the Black Witch, in Mahlke's case, the cat, has to be found. In that sense he is a continuation of Oskar. On the other hand he is also a reversal of Oskar. Whereas Oskar avoided the world, Mahlke's greatest ambition is to become part of it, irrespective of its perversity. When Oskar attempted to become a 'useful member of society' it was *after* the collapse of National

6. Luzi Rennwand, member of the Duster gang in *TD*.

Socialism; Mahlke's desperate attempts at integration take place within a National Socialist society.

Oskar undergoes three distinct stages in his moral development, each representing an advance on the previous one. Mahlke's development is a regressive one, for his moral awareness is sharpest at the beginning of the story. In his adolescence he distinguishes himself as a person of exceptional integrity. When his schoolmates eat seagull droppings and stage their public orgies of masturbation, Mahlke alone abstains. He is an excellent pupil, without being a 'swot', and always stands up for those in need: not only does he come to the rescue of a blind teacher by removing the condom from the door handle, specially put there for the latter's annoyance, but he even risks his own life when saving a younger schoolboy from drowning.

Unfortunately, Mahlke's sensitivity in the private sphere does not extend to the political one. His rebellion against the cat degenerates into a senseless ambition to outdo his classmates at all costs without considering the value of his objectives. The shock of the cat's attack is so great that it blunts Mahlke's perspicacity instead of sharpening it. Mahlke's failure is on no account due to his entering the fight, but only to the way he goes about it. His revolt is not the product of personal reflection, as Oskar's is; it is built on a foundation taken over unquestioningly from outside.

Whereas Oskar knowingly steps outside society, Mahlke's greatest desire is to conform. Oskar chooses to be an outsider, Mahlke is forced into the position. His family background, his old-fashioned clothes inherited from his father, not to mention his physical peculiarities mark him out. An abnormally large Adam's apple crowns his distinctiveness, a visible manifestation of all Mahlke's strength and weakness.

Thus Oskar's and Mahlke's physical abnormalities are of a very different order. Oskar's deformation is self-inflicted, Mahlke's is an involuntary one. His protruding Adam's apple is only a handicap, whereas Oskar's disguise as a three-year-old is a deliberate camouflage. Oskar fought his society by opposing it with his own brand of morality. Mahlke simply adopts the National Socialist scale of values. By reaching out for the highest military honour that the regime has to offer, Mahlke enslaves himself to its moral code.

29

Oskar *seems* to choose the line of least resistance, yet in practice he achieves more than Mahlke, who makes life as difficult for himself as possible. Swimming is a case in point. Pilenz tells us that before Mahlke could swim he was only half a human being. What Pilenz does not say, however, is that Mahlke's swimming is not only a springboard to success, but also to complete failure. What starts off as a promising act of emancipation, turns into an act of self-annihilation.

The reason for this must be sought in Mahlke's Adam's apple. It is not simply a physical defect, but the externalisation of an acute vulnerability. The very first page of the novella is loaded with such symbolic overtones: 'the . . . black cat tensed for a leap . . .'[7] for Mahlke's Adam's apple had become the cat's mouse'.[8] When the aggression of the cat is imminent, Pilenz actually helps it on its way:

> I . . . seized the cat and showed it Mahlke's mouse: and Joachim Mahlke let out a yell. . . .[9]

Mahlke's outcry is like a shudder of recognition that the time has come for him to face up to the world. His outcry is followed by positive action; at first his activities are centred around the school world, then he turns to the world of adults. Initially he evolves a whole series of appeasers, but none of his chosen devices seem to pacify the 'mouse'. Only the Virgin Mary proves a source of strength.

> Whatever he did, from diving to his subsequent military accomplishments, was done for her, or else . . . to distract attention from his Adam's apple. And perhaps, in addition to Virgin and mouse, there was yet a third motive: Our school . . . and particularly the auditorium, meant a great deal to Joachim Mahlke.[10]

Symbolism Pilenz states in this paragraph the three key motifs of the novella:

7. *CM.* p. 5.
8. *CM.* p. 6.
9. *CM.* p. 6.
10. *CM.* pp. 34–5.

the Adam's apple as the mouse, the school as the cat, and the Virgin Mary as one who tries, yet fails to reconcile these two antagonistic forces (the significance of Mahlke's catholicism will be discussed later). The school alone, the cause of all Mahlke's humiliations, could have restored his balance. The conclusion of this unhappy ambition has already been anticipated.

The Adam's apple is not only the key to the novella, it is also the link between the universal and the political levels. It is, as so many of Grass's symbols, a 'private' symbol which assumes political dimensions because of its historical context. Mahlke is interested only in alleviating a private grievance—he is unaware of the political implications of his acts as his comment on the first war speech demonstrates:

> Now they need a bag of forty if they want the medal.
> At the beginning and after they were through in
> France and in the North, it only took twenty—if it
> keeps on like this. . . .[11]

When he bemoans the escalation from twenty to forty planes, far from dissociating himself from the increase in human sacrifice, he laments the escalation in effort and courage required to obtain the Knight's cross. Only this type of acclaim would help him come to terms with his Adam's apple. By the time of the second speech, Mahlke steals the medal to try out its effect:

> For the first time the Adam's apple . . . slumbered
> beneath his skin. For a time it had no need to move,
> for the harmonious cross . . . soothed it. . . .[12]

Mahlke overcomes his moral reservations about the military ethos, because his need to conform is stronger than his misgivings. Thus Mahlke remains only a *potential* protester.[13] He has himself expelled from the Young Folk, not because he objects to Hitler,

11. *CM.* p. 51.
12. *CM.* p. 80.
13. The opposite view has been put forward by John Reddick, who maintains that Mahlke sees through the corruption of his society and fights it on his terms, cf. 'Eine epische Trilogie des Leidens', *Text und Kritik* 1/1a, 1971, pp. 42 ff.

but because the meeting interfered with the early Mass. When serving in the army he writes to his ailing mother: 'Sometimes I begin to wonder what it is all for,' but he is just as quick to allay his doubts: 'but I suppose it has to be.'[14] Any direct criticism of the Third Reich is either articulated by the narrator or even more directly, is rooted within the language itself.

The German critic Holthusen has characterised Grass's language in *Cat and Mouse* as a political instrument.[15] The first example that springs to mind is the strict avoidance of the word 'Knight's cross' up to the very last page. By calling it a 'lozenge', 'hardware', 'iron biscuit', the 'exact opposite of an onion', a 'galvanised four-leaf clover', an 'I-will-not-utter-it', Grass expresses his contempt for the medal. Other passages where language is used as a political instrument are Klohse's introductions of the two lieutenants where his choice of words extols the Spartan virtues, ideals of purity and subordination to the community, conveyed in flowery clichés. The speeches of the 'heroes' themselves abound in such inarticulate sentimentalities, glossed over with verbose descriptions of nature, for instance

> the foaming wake follows the boat which, swathed like a bride in festive veils of spray, strides onward to the marriage of death. . . .

Pilenz concludes his account:

> . . . in the ensuing metaphor the bride was obliterated.[16]

Mahlke senses the insincerity of these speeches, but, unlike Oskar, he seems incapable of grasping that his own idea of heroism, as exemplified to him by his father, for instance, is incompatible with the National Socialist ethos. In the 'Faith, Hope, Love' chapter, Oskar laments the debasement of Christian values. Mahlke, on the other hand, has no difficulty in making his catholicism coexist with his activities in the Nazi navy.

No character in Grass's entire oeuvre is as completely a

14. *CM.* p. 103.

15. H. E. Holthusen, 'Günter Grass als politischer Autor', *Der Monat*, no. 216, 1966, pp. 66–81.

16. *CM.* pp. 64–5.

victim as Mahlke. He is firstly a victim of himself, that is of his compulsive urge to compensate for extreme insecurity by extreme self-assertion, and secondly he is a victim of a society which takes advantage of his maladjustment. Not only does the system exploit his physical courage and extraordinary will-power, but in the end it refuses to grant him the recognition for which he has fought so tenaciously. Mahlke is unaware of this exploitation. If anything, he has the mistaken belief that he is the one who uses the system, in order to alleviate his personal grievance: his Adam's apple.

Grass originally planned *Cat and Mouse* as an integral part of *Dog Years*, but later perceived it as an artistic entity in its own right. It is clearly a transitional work in that it carries on themes and characters of *The Tin Drum*, whilst at the same time prefiguring *Dog Years*. If one looks at the status of the characters in the trilogy, all of them are victims to a greater or lesser degree. But Oskar only pretends to be a victim; Amsel, one of the main protagonists of *Dog Years* knows how to turn persecution into success; only Matern, the other protagonist of *Dog Years* is comparable to Mahlke, or, to put it differently, Mahlke is Matern and Amsel in one. Mahlke is reminiscent of Amsel, because, as far as society is concerned, being a Jew is comparable to sporting a large Adam's apple—both are social handicaps inflicted on their bearers. Both Amsel and Mahlke spend their whole lives fighting for their respective ambitions and both are prepared to cooperate with the system to further their goals. Amsel collects money for the Nazis and is happiest when donning an SA uniform; Mahlke, as we know, goes the whole way. What they have in common is a desire to shake off their otherness and merge with the masses. But whereas Amsel joins in with the full knowledge of his deviousness, Mahlke does so in relative innocence.

Matern of *Dog Years* is also a victim, although, in contrast to Mahlke, his handicaps are all psychological. He is more socially aware than Mahlke, but, like him, lacks political judgment. Their self-importance and utter lack of humour is another common feature. They are both fanatics. Whereas Amsel's and Oskar's aloofness seems to verge on opportunism but is in fact its very opposite, Mahlke's and Matern's intransigence, suspiciously reminiscent of moral fibre, eventually leads them to the worst type

33

of opportunism. In the case of Matern, this opportunism takes the form of an attempted murder on his friend Amsel.

Treachery in friendship is another theme that links *Cat and Mouse* to *Dog Years*. Mahlke prefigures only half of Matern, the other half is foreshadowed by the narrator, Pilenz. Both Pilenz and Matern are treacherous friends and both are persecuted by their treachery throughout their adult lives. Pilenz has this to say about his relationship to Mahlke:

> I spend whole nights discussing . . . with the Franciscan
> Father Alban . . . I tell him about Mahlke and
> Mahlke's Virgin, Mahlke's throat and Mahlke's aunt,
> Mahlke's sugar water, the parting in the middle of
> his hair, his gramophone, snowy owl, screwdriver,
> woollen pompoms, luminous buttons, about cat and
> mouse and *mea culpa*. [17]

The ambivalent love-hate relationship between Matern and Amsel, German and Jew, is symbolised by a pen-knife in *Dog Years*. The knife is paralleled in *Cat and Mouse* by Mahlke's tin-opener. But, unlike the knife, which re-emerges, the tin-opener is swallowed up by the sea. In the same way that Amsel surfaces again, Mahlke does not. Because the outsider Mahlke is not a Jew like Amsel, the political overtones of his friendship with Pilenz are not as explicit; yet Pilenz undoubtedly plays the role of the German persecutor, assuming, after the event, the role of expiator.

If Mahlke is an anticipation of the two characters Amsel and Matern, Pilenz also prefigures two characters of *Dog Years*. Pilenz's part as a friend and betrayer parallels that of Matern. Temperamentally he foreshadows one of the narrators of *Dog Years*, Harry Liebenau. They resemble each other in their indecisiveness and lack of originality, in absorbing and receiving without ever creating or giving; both are atheists and wish they were believers.

Another character linking all three novels is Tulla: she makes her first appearance in *The Tin Drum* as the ominous triangular-faced Luzi Rennwand, the Black Witch being her mythical

17. *CM.* p. 78.

34

antecedent. Her ghost is resurrected in *Cat and Mouse* as the full-blooded Tulla, a female creature mainly instrumental in challenging and admiring the virility of the pubescent Conradinum crowd. Apart from that, her role is peripheral; it comes nowhere near her status as the incarnation of amorality in *Dog Years*.

At the beginning of the discussion we called *Cat and Mouse* both a concentrate and a continuation of *The Tin Drum*. So far this has been illustrated by investigating how the characters of the three novels interact with one another. In *The Tin Drum*, Oskar's lament was mainly centred on man's wilful misinterpretation of the notions of the Epistle to the Corinthians; his protest was thus directed against vast areas of human behaviour. In *Cat and Mouse* the author focuses on the symptoms of a sick society: the Knight's cross is one of them. Unmasking the much-admired courage of one who has been awarded the medal for a particularly expert exercise in human slaughter is a more specialised line of attack than were the anti-war innuendoes in *The Tin Drum*. In *Cat and Mouse* Grass may have limited his protest, but by limiting it, he has also intensified it.

The same process of specialisation applies to the other two prominent themes of the novella: the Church and the school. Oskar illustrates how human nature is capable of twisting and turning Christian principles in order to fit its own selfish ends. This 'pick and choose' attitude, to which the Catholic dogma lays itself open, is best exemplified by Mahlke, who concentrates all his fervour on to the Virgin Mary. Otherwise he is indifferent, if not hostile to the Christian faith:

Religion

> Of course I don't believe in God. He's just a swindle to stultify the people. The only thing I believe in is the Virgin Mary.[18]

Virgin Mary

Mahlke exemplifies how such a selective attitude, if taken to extremes, eventually leads to the total separation of Catholic symbols from their religious context. To Mahlke, the Virgin Mary represents the ideal woman, he uses her as a vessel for all his fantasies, sexual and otherwise.

The fact that Mahlke can make her bend to all his desires

18. *CM.* p. 120.

35

Just as Matson focused on one poetic theme & ideology, so did Stehlke.

makes her, initially, a genuine protector of Mahlke's mouse and all its painful implications. But her strength also constitutes her weakness. Chosen by Mahlke to reconcile the cat with the mouse, she fails. At the beginning, she isolates the protagonist from his National Socialist surroundings. But when Mahlke switches camps, she does too. His visions on the battlefield are inspired by her. National Socialism is not the cause, but the consequence of Mahlke's religious aberrations, *wandering* his uncritical cult of a catholic idol simply deteriorates into another 'ism', another ideology. Ideological links between the religious and the military pervade the novella throughout. Mallenbrandt, for instance, one of the minor 'cats' in the story, teaches not only religion, but also physical education. Another example is the interchangeability between the gymnasium and the chapel. Pilenz makes these cross-references repeatedly, when he writes about the 'gymnasium quality of this church' and the 'tall-windowed gymnasium ... topped with a tarred wooden cross'.

The third and final aspect of society attacked in this novella is the school; here again Grass is singling out one particular institution of society. Klohse as its principal is as perfect an impersonation of the cat as possible. Pilenz, another upholder of the cat mentality, is the first to recognise it in others. When the decorated Mahlke returns to his old school in the hope of delivering his speech, Pilenz actually casts Klohse in the role of the cat.[19] In his feline fashion, Klohse does not congratulate Mahlke on his achievements, but simply suggests that he should give the talk at the school to which he was transferred after his expulsion. The rambling officialese characterising the style of the school's justification for barring Mahlke from the coveted auditorium only disguises the inhumanity of the pedagogue responsible for Mahlke's disappearance.

When Mahlke takes his revenge on Klohse by striking him, the slapped man 'stood stiff as a ramrod ... embodying the school ... the Conradinian spirit, the Conradinum.'[20] Not so Mahlke. This revenge brings about his final collapse. It is Mahlke's tragedy that he himself is unaware of the legitimacy of his active defence—only the reader can welcome his act as an act of rebellion.

19. *CM.* p. 124.
20. *CM.* p. 119.

Mahlke's mask a prey to 'cats' - Pilenz & Klohse, & their ideological acknowledge in National Socialism.

4   *Dog Years*

In *Cat and Mouse* Pilenz refers to *Dog Years* (1963), the last of the 'Danzig trilogy', in connection with Brunies's deportation, by calling it 'a dismal, complicated story, which deserved to be written, but somewhere else, not by me, and certainly not in connection with Mahlke.'[1]

Dog Years, as the title implies, is indeed, a 'dismal, complicated story', and not only with reference to the teacher, foster father and Nazi victim, Brunies. Dismal, because, even more ferociously than in the previous two novels, it unmasks the inhumanity of a social, political and philosophical system and its dehumanising effect on a whole society; complicated, because this is no longer the account of a relatively intelligible world, as reproduced by the narrators Oskar and Pilenz.

Such intelligibility is severely challenged in *Dog Years*: the omniscient narrator has made way for three or rather four narrators memorising and relating events, each from his own perspective. This structural change is by no means a gimmick or a framework superimposed from outside, as suggested by some critics.[2] It reflects a profound distrust of the capacity of one single individual to grasp the truth. The juxtaposition of the three narrators, Brauxel, Harry and Matern, has two main functions. Firstly, it evokes a simultaneity of experience telescoping past and present; secondly it acts as a mutual corrective and thus encourages the reader to piece together for himself a true picture of reality from the inconsistencies of the three parts. This one can only do after having read the whole novel, which demands that one should be critical throughout. The fourth narrator is none other than Grass himself, who steps in at the end of

1. *CM.* p. 38.
2. See for example W. Jens, 'Das Pandämonium des Günter Grass', *Die Zeit,* 6 September, 1963.

the second part, with the gruesome yet true tale of the mound of bones.

In style and mood, *Dog Years* is close to *The Tin Drum*; ethically, that is in its acceptance of moral responsibility, this last novel of the trilogy represents an extension of its predecessors. Tripartite structure, and allocation of time (pre-war, war and post-war period) are common both to *The Tin Drum* and *Dog Years*. Brauksel is the author of the first section 'Morning Shifts', the title referring both to his present occupation as the director of a mine, and to his account of the first formative experiences of Amsel and Matern, the bottom layer on which the whole of the novel unfolds. (The double meaning is more easily recognisable in the German word 'Frühschichten'.) At this stage one does not know that the narrator Brauksel, alias Brauxel, is in fact Amsel himself, hero of 'Morning Shifts', although, as the self-acknowledged head of the team of authors, he insinuates foreknowledge of the other two accounts.

The novel opens significantly with a pocket-knife parable, consistently linking past and present. It introduces us to the teeth-grinding Walter Matern throwing the same knife into the Vistula, with which he had sworn bloodbrotherhood to his friend Amsel. We are told of Matern's Catholic family background, his paralysed grandmother, her resurrection on his baptism, and his father, the deaf but clairvoyant miller Matern, who is able to prophecy the future with the help of meal-worms. The Matern Dog, Senta, and her 'promising' genealogy, punctuates the symbolically loaded tale of the never untroubled friendship between the two boys.

Brauksel—for this is essential to his political purpose—also delves into his own family history (as did Oskar who thought his background essential to his own biography), before introducing himself as the young scarecrow artist, Amsel. Both Walter Matern's and Eddi Amsel's childhoods are framed by the ever-present Vistula 'growing constantly broader in memory'. Brauksel's main function as the head of the author consortium is to mobilise the memory of his fellow narrators for obvious educational purposes. Born one month later than Matern, Amsel sketches in his parents' peculiarities, which account largely for his own idiosyncrasies. Amsel's father had a talent for amassing money and, even after his father's death, Amsel's mother distinguishes herself by her aptitude for business. Amsel prevaricates about his father's origin: 'Of course Amsel was not a Jew', and contradicts himself a few pages later: 'Who can tell whether Albrecht Amsel, merchant and reserve lieutenant, wasn't a Jew after all?'[3] explaining his prevarications with the far-reaching remark 'for all origins are what we choose to make of them',[4] and therefore, paradoxically, 'of course Albrecht Amsel was a Jew'.[5] What Albrecht Amsel chose to make of his origins is well known: namely to 'overcome' his semitic blood (with the help of the fanatic anti-semite Jewish philosopher, Otto Weininger) and display all possible so-called Aryan virtues, such as playing sports and singing, crowning his 'Germanness' with his death on the battlefield at Verdun. 'Amsel henceforth kept about him Otto Weininger's extraordinary book'; even at the time of writing Brauksel acknowledges his indebtedness, for 'Weininger has grafted quite a few ideas on to the present writer. The scarecrow is created in man's image.'[6]

Even before his encounter with Weininger, Amsel's Protestant baptism marks him out as a born scarecrow builder, and the novel is described by him as 'this handbook on the construction of effective scarecrows.'[7] It was 'Amsel's keen sense of reality ... which provided his products with closely observed detail, which made them functional and crow-repellent',[8] although the narrator stresses throughout that Amsel's creatures were built 'for no purpose and with no enemy in view.'[9] He models his art first on people, then on nature, then links both in his grandiose 'half willow, half grandmother' production, moving on to Prussian mythology, and finally specialising in uniformed, preferably SA scarecrows with a built-in mechanism that would make them as true-to-life as possible.

His friend Matern, SA man himself, does not appreciate these artefacts and thanks Amsel for the verisimilitude by beating him

3. *DY*. p. 35.
4. *DY*. p. 35.
5. *DY*. p. 35.
6. *DY*. p. 37.
7. *DY*. p. 38.
8. *DY*. p. 39.
9. *DY*. p. 39.

up and rolling him into a snowman. This episode is related to us by Harry Liebenau, author of Book Two. Harry's 'Love Letters' are addresssed to his cousin Tulla, 'more a something than a girl'. Before involving us in Amsel's 'snow miracle', Harry engrosses himself in the history of the dog Harras, who had sired Prinz, who was given to the 'Führer' as a birthday present. Harry also tells us of Brunies's gypsy foster-daughter and her dramatic rise to prima ballerina, which parallels Eddi Amsel's metamorphosis into Haseloff Goldmouth.

Harry's memory, although comprehensive, is that of an aesthete. He is such an able writer, that even the most atrocious events dissolve into language when rendered by his pen. The history of the affluent town of Stutthof is recounted, separated only by a colon from the chilling phrase 'and between 1939 and 1945 in Stutthof Concentration Camp . . . people died, I don't know how many.'[10] Little wonder that Grass feels impelled to interrupt Harry's skilled but non-committal narrative and to contrast it with his own terse version of the 'pile of bones', framed by the musically contrived discourse on purity.[11] This transitional passage leads on to a concentrated attack on the German philosopher Heidegger's existentialist jargon, in which most of the events during the war period, including the German capitulation, are couched.

The 'Materniads' presents the last version of a painful past, with one of its main victims, Matern, as its chronicler. If Brauksel invoked the Vistula as the river of remembrance, Matern conjures up Lethe as one of forgetfulness. He can only delve into other people's pasts and excels in wholesale condemnation. When it comes to his own sins, his memory abandons him. Brauksel's exhortations leave him untouched, he storms forward in his campaign of vengeance, including in his diatribe against the Nazi dog years, the 'worm-ridden' capitalistic period of the 'economic miracle'. The novel is concluded by the long-awaited reunion of Matern with Amsel-Haseloff-Goldmouth-Brauksel, who presents Matern with the lost pocket-knife, but Matern, clenching his fist as before, throws it away a second time. Brauksel

10. *DY.* p. 295.
11. *DY.* p. 322.

takes Matern on a guided tour of his scarecrow mine, but fails to make his friend and persecutor see light.

In spite of the fundamental structural differences between *The Tin Drum* and *Dog Years*, the latter novel reflecting a far more complex and fragmented view of the world, there are significant thematic links—religious and political—which make us call the third novel an extension of its two predecessors. Matern, like Oskar and Mahlke, is irresistibly drawn to the Virgin Mary, but his final rejection of her is more radical than theirs ever was; so is Matern's eventual rejection of Catholicism, as this explicit accusation of a Catholic dignitary illustrates:

> 'And it was you, you and no one else, who said that, get back into the SA. A lot of rubbish about the concordat and anecdotes from Maria Laach. They even secretly blessed a banner and whined out prayers for the Führer. . . . And to me, Matern, you said: My son, resume the brown garment of honour. Jesus Christ who died on the cross . . . has sent us the Führer to stamp out the seed of the godless with your help and mine.'[12]

Where Oskar is still concerned with testing God's power by his symbolical drumming contests, Matern's grudge is far more tangible: he accuses the Catholic Church of direct collaboration.

This more pronounced historical awareness is further exemplified in Grass's treatment of the Stauffenberg plot. The officers' revolt is only given a perfunctory mention in *The Tin Drum*; in *Dog Years* the theme is elaborated over five pages, in which the 'would-be assassin' Stauffenberg is taken to task for having 'neglected to go the whole hog',[13] because 'he tried to save himself for great tasks after a successful assassination'.[14] 'To sum it up', writes the narrator Grass, 'the assassin was a dud'.[15] Had Stauffenberg seriously planned to assassinate Hitler, Grass argues rather simplistically, he would have been prepared to sacrifice his own

12. *DY*. pp. 440–1.
13. *DY*. p. 356.
14. *DY*. p. 356.
15. *DY*. p. 357.

life. Furthermore, the author is determined to unveil the plot as a reactionary rebellion, inspired solely by the desire to save Germany's honour before total collapse.

When dealing with the persecution of the Jews, Grass is just as explicit. In *The Tin Drum* the brutalities of the SA were exemplified by Markus's suicide and Fajngold's hallucinations. In *Dog Years* the horrors of the extermination camps are allegorised in the mountain of bones throughout fourteen pages. This fairy-tale-like incantation is couched in Heidegger's jargon, so as to contrast the philosopher's mystical terminology with its concrete political consequences.

Another symbol reappearing as an allegory in *Dog Years* is the transformation of the Black Witch into a dog, finishing up as Hitler's dog, Prinz. In both instances, the pile of bones and the dog, there is a move towards greater rationality in the name of didacticism. The intention is further underlined by Grass's introduction of cultural material, which gives the novel an intellectual dimension absent in *The Tin Drum*. Oskar saw Goethe and Rasputin as projections of himself, but Amsel and Matern are governed by their mentors. Amsel endeavours to be a living refutation of Weininger's antisemitic theories, and Matern is a victim of Heidegger's philosophy. Through them, Grass wants to expose the intrinsic dangers of the German idealist philosophy as a fertile breeding ground for authoritarian modes of thinking.

The Tin Drum indicates in its title the central position of art in this novel. *Dog Years* should, by analogy, merely bear witness to a time of political upheaval. But the title *Dog Years* reflects only part of the contents. In this novel, scarecrows are the most significant symbol, reflecting, as dynamic products of art, the various stages of an historical process. With the advent of National Socialism, the scarecrow develops from a dialectical symbol of Amsel's art into an allegory of a political ideology. The same applies to miller Matern's worms, a private fantasy before the war which assumes public importance after it.

In the development of the scarecrow symbol, three separate phases, coinciding with the divisions of the novel, can be distinguished. Initially, Amsel models his creations on people and nature, linking both in one of his most awe-inspriing projects, the half-willow, half-grandmother scarecrow, which proves so terrifying to men and animals alike that Amsel is forced into destroying it, which leads him to the following insight:

> Thus it was brought home to an artist for the first time, that, when his works embodied a close enough study of nature, they had power not only over the birds of heaven, but . . . were also capable of disorganising the tranquil rural gait . . . of a human being.[16]

Next comes Amsel's obsession with Prussian militarism and mythology which is firmly rooted in his encounter with the ideas of Otto Weininger, as propounded in the notorious book, *Sex and Character*. The chapter responsible for Amsel's obsession is that on Judaism, from which whole paragraphs are directly quoted in *Dog Years*.[17] Weininger is an example of extreme self-hatred. To him Judaism is primarily a 'mental state' and not an unalterable racial one, which prompts him to urge all Jews to try and overcome their Jewishness.

> . . . the world-historical significance and enormous achievement of Jewry consists solely in this: in having continually brought the Aryan to consciousness of his self, in having reminded him of himself. . . . It is for this that the Aryan owes the Jew a debt of gratitude; thanks to him he knows what to guard against: against Jewishness as a possibility in himself.[18]

And because Weininger claims that the Jew neither sings nor engages in sports, Amsel, like his father before him, not only joins the choir, not only turns himself into a master faustball player, but also adopts his father's passion for all things Prussian. During that period Amsel's scarecrows celebrate the old Prussian gods Perkunos, Pikollos and Potrimpos, so that the scarecrows, far from being mere symbols of art, gradually come to represent National Socialist ideals. Like the drum, the scarecrows are dialectical, in that they represent ideology from the outside, as

16. *DY*. p. 58.
17. *DY*. pp. 202 ff. for example.
18. *DY*. p. 202.

well as denouncing it from the inside. But Amsel's time being what it is, his products are hailed as 'treasures of naïve yet formally mature folk art' in which the 'spirit of the Vikings and Christian simplicity in an East-German symbiosis' are 'flowering fresh and anew.'[19]

Amsel's most ambitious creation, which concludes the first phase of his artistic development, is to be a monument to the paradoxical nature of his craft: 'he was going to create a scarecrow in the form of a giant bird'.[20] But, the effect of this 'Great Cuckoo Bird' causes such terror that, together with the whole arsenal of scarecrows, it has to be destroyed. The burning of the scarecrows evokes the book burning operated by the National Socialists at the same time, especially as the 'autodafé', the 'great holocaust', is equally accompanied by antisemitic noises.

When Amsel acted on his first insight concerning the effects of his products, he was also prepared to sacrifice his artistic principles. The present destruction, however, is only a concession in name, not in substance. Amsel only conforms to the pressures of society outwardly; inwardly there is a growing determination to spite the restrictiveness of his political surroundings with his art, for the fire 'kindled all sorts of kindling in Amsel's little head and produced a fire that was never again to be quenched.'[21]

Amsel's second scarecrow phase, for which he adopts the more craftsman-like term of figures, contains more and more political innuendoes, as the following key passage illustrates, in which he contrasts his own intentions with those of society:

> Eddi Amsel built no scarecrows to ward off the sparrows . . . he built with no adversary in mind, on formal grounds. At the most he wished to convince a dangerously productive environment of his own productivity.[22]

Far from confirming Amsel's alleged belief in aestheticism, this postulate proves the very opposite, for with the modification 'at

19. *DY*. p. 68.
20. *DY*. p. 92.
21. *DY*. p. 98.
22. *DY*. p. 200.

the most . . .' Amsel is not only qualifying but positively negating any claim to mere formalism. The fact that Amsel is prepared to oppose his 'dangerously productive environment' with 'his own productivity' is the strongest commitment to be expected from an artist living under a totalitarian regime. His decision to capitalise on the political potential of his art results in scarecrow 'SA men who could march and salute, because they had a mechanism in their tummies'.[23] These turn out to be an anticipation of nine real-life Nazi 'scarecrows', who make it their business to knock Amsel down, with Walter Matern as their most active member. Amsel's metamorphosis, symbolic for the immortality of art, is paralleled by that of his artistic counterpart, the ballet dancer Jenny, who has been subjected to similar tortures and, like Amsel, has emerged victorious.

The history of the scarecrows reaches its climax with the 'scarecrow ballet'. Nowhere are artistic and political connotations so closely interwoven. The three figures in the ballet, the gardener, the gardener's daughter and the scarecrow, each symbolise the fundamental issues of the novel; that is, the interaction between art, society and politics with the daughter (played by Jenny) as the aesthete, the gardener as downtrodden pre-war German society and the scarecrows as political ideologists.

The ballet thus introduces the final phase of the scarecrow history, in that its meaning moves further and further away from art and becomes gradually identified with totalitarianism. This shift of emphasis is best exemplified by the scarecrows' totally unconnected reapparance on Matern's journey to the German Democratic Republic:

> . . . for scarecrows know no borders: parallel to
> Matern, the scarecrow message journeys to the
> Peaceloving Camp, shakes off the dust, leaves capitalistic
> rye behind it, is taken up by class-conscious
> scarecrows in socialised oats . . .[24]

More directly than elsewhere the scarecrow is here both the representation and the rejection of ideology. Its grotesqueness

23. *DY.* p. 225.
24. *DY.* p. 555.

45

reveals the corruption of the model it depicts. Whenever it occurs, one knows that the narrator is attacking a regime where doctrinaire thinking is prevalent.

Dog Years ends in the savage finale of the scarecrow hell, where instinctive, intellectual, political and scientific man are all unmasked with the same acrimony. Thus, in the inferno, the scarecrows' significance from art (phase one), to ideology (phase two) has been enlarged again to encompass the grotesqueness of all human endeavours (phase three).

Having dealt with Amsel, Weininger and the scarecrows, it is now necessary to point to their corollaries in Matern, Heidegger and the dog. The dog complements visually what Grass's version of Heidegger tries to achieve intellectually – scarecrow and dog undergo the same process of politicisation. The dog has a structural and a thematic function. Structurally it links the Amsel–Matern story with the Tulla-Harry-Jenny story; thematically, it functions as the living evidence of a perverse political system. But this degree of explicitness is only manifest in the third generation, Prinz, whose future political career is hinted at from the first page onwards. Senta, the first generation, except for her much emphasised blackness, seems a 'normal' family dog. With Harras the emphasis changes, he is not only black, but he is of 'pure Germanic descent'. Further evidence of his connection with National Socialism is Matern's poisoning of him as a 'Catholic Nazihog', as is Harras's intimate relationship with Tulla. For Tulla's birth coincides with a juncture point in politics, heralding the rise of the NSDAP, the persecution of the Jews and the imminent publication of Heidegger's *Time and Being*.[25]

Harras's so-called political career begins with Prinz. In Book Three, dog and scarecrow are reduced to an allegory of National Socialism, especially after Prinz has survived the collapse of the Third Reich as Pluto (demonstrating the survival of the Fascist and totalitarian mentalities in the post-war era), underlined by Pluto relentlessly persecuting Matern, and his final rejuvenation in East Germany.

The interweaving of the dog motif and the Heidegger parody is densest in the description of Prinz's flight after the German defeat; this is the most explicit episode in its equation of Hei-

25. *DY.* p. 126.

degger's jargon, the military National Socialist jargon and the dog's activities. Here is an example of such a linguistic mixture:

> 'Twelfth Army will manifest counter-tonality to fusty atonality of Reichcapital. Unburdenings of Being in Steglitz and southern edge of Tempelhof Airfield will project advanced selfpoint. The final struggle of the German people will be conducted with regard to the Nothing attuned to distantiality.'[26]

The 'Nothing attuned to distantiality' is no other than Hitler's dog Prinz. 'Unburdenings of Being' is merely a euphemism for murder. This is **Grass's** way of expressing his contempt for National Socialist objectives: putting the Germans' battle for survival on the same level as the capturing of Hitler's Alsatian.

Grass attacks Heidegger on two inter-related grounds. The first concerns the philospher's flirtations with the Hitler regime, when, as Matern reminds us, Heidegger disowned his Jewish mentor, Husserl, at a time when help was most needed. The second concerns his philosophical jargon. The characters admiring and using Heidegger's terminology are Störtebecker, Harry Liebenau and Matern, all of them desperately longing for a system of belief, yet incapable of devising one of their own. Grass's discourse on purity prefaces his polemics against Heidegger; it reveals his fundamental distrust of absolutes, as postulated by the philosopher's idealism, and especially his distrust of the concept of authenticity. The term in Grass's view is totally devoid of any social or political content, it simply means to be fully what one is, irrespective of ethical justification.

Authenticity in action on a political level is illustrated by the systematic extermination of rats, the rats here standing for the Jews:

> And when thought forsook metaphysics. . . . And when the rats left the ship. . . . When they attacked even infants and old people riveted to their chairs. . . .[27]

26. *DY*. p. 377.
27. *DY*. p. 328.

All these descriptions, with the smoke emanating from the near-by Stutthof concentration camp, are generously endowed with Heidegger's terminology. The clipped syntax makes nonsense of it, but the contrasting effect between verbose pomposity and dehumanisation is maintained throughout.

On a private level, the concept of authenticity has equally disastrous consequences. Matern defines it as 'freedom is freedom to the I': to put it more bluntly, his understanding of Heidegger legitimates boundless egotism. When he wants to rid himself of his self-inflicted responsibility towards Inge, he seeks to exculpate himself in Heidegger's 'strange words':

> 'I essent . . . I, source of grounding! I, possibility—soil—identification! I, GROUND, GROUNDING IN THE GROUNDLESS!' Ingemouse learns the meaning of these obscure words shortly before Christmas. . . . He shoves off. . . .[28]

From the concept of authenticity Heidegger derives his glorification of death that leads him to the celebration of sacrifice. When Störtebecker, Harry and Matern find themselves face to face with the irrefutable reality of a pile of human bones, Störte-becker's answer has been ready for weeks:

> 'We must conceive of piledupness in the openness of Being, the divulgation of care, and endurance to death as the consummate essence of existence.'[29]

and he concludes 'with a grandiose gesture of blessing':

'There lies the essence-ground of all history.'[30] Such an oracle reveals what Grass denounces in Heidegger's thought: the uncritical sanctification of history, which according to Grass also links Heidegger's philosophy to that of older German idealists notably of Hegel, who interpreted history as the manifestation of the 'Spirit'.

28. *DY.* p. 411.
29. *DY.* p. 334.
30. *DY.* p. 334.

Harry Liebenau, wise after the event, explains what the Heidegger parody is about, when he writes:

> A boy, a young man, a uniformed high school student who venerated the Führer . . . and . . . the philosopher Martin Heidegger. With the help of these models he succeeded in burying a real mound made of human bones under medieval allegories. The pile of bones, which in reality cried out to high heaven . . . was mentioned in his diary as a place of sacrifice, erected in order that purity might come-to-be in the luminous, which transluminates purity and so fosters light.[31]

Mystifying, priest-like language, pomposity, vagueness and irrationality, finally its dangerous irrelevance to the political demands of our time—these are the basic tenets of Grass's line of attack.

If the first critics of *The Tin Drum* were outraged by its immorality, critics of *Dog Years*, on the contrary, were shocked by its obtrusive didacticism. They were particularly upset by Grass's use of imagery. The scarecrow and the dog have already been discussed. The knife is another image, symbolising the love-hate relationship between German and Jew (although Amsel is only half Jewish). Being for ever retrievable, it signifies the necessity for co-existence. George Steiner interprets the depiction of the German-Jewish conflict in *Dog Years* as the 'neurotic conjecture of some secret, fore-doomed relationship between Nazi and Jew, of a hidden fraternity or mutual fascination deeper than the outward show of loathing and destruction.'[32]

Far from paying tribute to the already existing mystical theory that love-hate is inevitable between German and Jew, Grass makes nonsense of the racist theory altogether. Amsel behaves like an 'exemplary Aryan',[33] thus refuting the idea that German and Jew are intrinsically different. What makes the Jew really different in the end is the constant reminder by society of his

31. *DY*. pp. 338–9.
32. George Steiner, *Language and Silence*, 1967, p. 133.
33. J. B. Neveux, 'Günter Grass le Vistulien', *Etudes Germaniques*, v. 21, p. 546.

49

alleged difference, as Sartre puts it: 'It is antisemitism which makes the Jew.'[34]

The dogs are linked to Matern, the scarecrows to Amsel, with the knife as the eternal connection between them. Then there are two more devices, one can hardly call them symbols, which serve a purely functional purpose: Miller Matern's worms are responsible for the corruption of the economic miracle in Germany. Finally there are the 'knowledge glasses' the only means by which Matern can be confronted with his own guilt.

Grass's exemplary use of imagery and characters, as opposed to a more idiosyncratic one in his two previous novels, deepens his analysis of National Socialism and its consequences for Germany. *The Tin Drum* ends with a forceful reminder of everybody's individual guilt, a guilt coupled with an equally obsessive fear. A large question mark hangs over the future. *Cat and Mouse* restricts itself to the war-time period, so the question of finding a *modus vivendi* in present-day Germany does not arise. In *Dog Years* the denunciation is strengthened by the suggestion that Hitler's role was not an inexplicable accident, but rather the result of totalitarian modes of thinking prevalent in German philosophy. Only by exposing the roots that nurture totalitarian regimes can their growth be prevented. This requires not only knowledge of the intellectual climate we live in, but also profound self-knowledge. Is that not the message of the concluding lines of the novel?

We're both naked. Each of us bathes by himself.[35]

34. Jean Paul Sartre, *Reflexions sur la question juive*, 1954, p. 61.
35. *DY.* p. 610.

5   The Writer as Political Activist

Each successive novel in the 'Danzig trilogy' represents an intensification of political awareness, a process evinced by Grass's use of narrative perspective, metaphors and treatment of themes. This evolution in Grass's literary practice was traced in the three previous chapters; his own deliberations on the relationship between literature and politics, as set out in his extra-literary output will now be discussed. In attempting this we shall first focus on the writer's political speeches,[1] then on his views on commitment in literature as expressed in his literary criticism[2] and finally discuss *The Plebeians Rehearse the Uprising*[3] as Grass's dramatic illustration of the conflict between writer and political activist.

In one of his lectures Grass complains that

> Students never weary of organising discussions revolving around questions like: 'Ought a writer to be committed?'[4]

To him this subject is nothing but an academic exercise, and obsessive preoccupation with it, no more than a cheap substitute for active participation in grassroot politics. Grass himself accepts only one definition of commitment: 'To engage oneself is . . . to act'.[5] And act he does and has done for the past decade, although both the tone and type of action have changed over that period. When he contributed to a pre-election paperback in

1. *SO.* (1969); *Dokumente zur politischen Wirkung*, (*GD.*) 1971.
2. *LD.* (1968).
3. *The Plebeians Rehearse the Uprising* with an introductory address ('Shakespeare Speech'), 1967 (*P.*).
4. 'On Writers as Court Jesters and on Non-existent Courts' in *SO.* p. 52.
5. 'Sich engagieren heisst frei übersetzt etwas tun', *Theater*, 1969, p. 14.

1961 (*The Alternative or Do we need a new Government*),[6] his support for the Social Democratic Party, the SPD, was at best tentative, with the party figuring as 'Auntie SPD', or 'bad conscience', whose election to office would represent no more than a 'faint hope' on his political horizon. In that same essay he taunts the electorate by promising that Oskar Matzerath's son and half-brother Kurt would also vote SPD, and comes to the sarcastic conclusion: 'one more proof how influential writers can be.'[7]

As if to defy this realistic insight into the limitations of a writer's political influence, he wrote at the same time to the East German author, Anna Seghers, urging her to protest against the erection of the Berlin Wall. In the same letter he openly appeals to her moral responsibility as a writer, by revealing to her how *The Seventh Cross*, Anna Seghers's best-known novel, had 'formed him' and 'sharpened his eye'.[8] This plea would suggest that Grass attributes to literature an important educational function.

But can Grass's emphasis on the political influence of other people's literature be applied to his own production? Does his own work also represent a symbiosis between art and politics? And does this symbiosis, which we have sought to unravel, correspond to Grass's own view of himself? On very rare occasions —for remarks to the contrary are the rule—he alludes to a kind of unity between the two activities, when he says, for instance, that his election speeches and his fiction are written with the same ink,[9] or that it is the same impulse that drives him into politics and literature.[10]

The impulse referred to is that of educating, enlightening, spreading reason—all leitmotifs of his 1965 election speeches. Then he set out as a private individual wanting to give a good example of 'civic initiative'—his status as a writer was supposed to be purely accidental. Consequently, apart from his indefatigable solicitations to political reason, a good deal of Grass's energies were spent in denigrating those colleagues who made

6. *Die Alternative oder Brauchen wir eine neue Regierung?*, 1961.
7. *GD.* p. 4.
8. *GD.* p. 6.
9. *GD.* p. 34.
10. *Der Spiegel*, No. 33, 1969, p. 94.

their public political stands in their capacity as writers. The following indictment stands for many:

> I condemn our high priests of blameless biography, who earn the ludicrous privilege of impersonating the conscience of the nation by writing articles for some semi-liberal newspaper. . . . And so they grind out their daring aphorisms and in their sheltered preserves expatiate . . . on freedom of thought, the problem of independence among intellectuals, and the difficulty of writing the truth. Dancing godlike over the exhaust fumes of our society, they diffuse their academic Marxism into the empyrean and turn their attention to the far-off misery of Indo-China and Persia, which, thanks to their intellectual elevation, they have no difficulty in understanding. They will turn out an interminable epic hymn to Fidel Castro and his sugar-cane island long before it would occur to them to shorten the legs of falsehood in their own country with a simple plea for Willy Brandt.[11]

As his speech gathers momentum, his polemics verge on vindictiveness. He summons his audience not to be taken in by this intellectual élite, these 'impersonators of Germany's conscience', because they have never descended to the people, but kept themselves in perfect purity, praising peace and condemning the atom bomb.

Grass projects himself as someone who does feel for the common man, as the down-to-earth political thinker who accepts the challenge of reality as his point of departure. The desire for absolutes he leaves to his utopian colleagues, whereas he himself chooses compromise as the essence of politically viable solutions. Pragmatism, a word of abuse to them, is a worth-while objective to him; it is not to be confounded with opportunism.

After extolling reason, he holds up tolerance as an equally desirable goal. It is in the name of tolerance that he spoke up for the re-establishment of the German Communist Party (which was still illegal in 1969) and warned against the banning of the

11. *SO.* p. 38.

neo-Nazi party, the NPD, which was then in the ascendancy, for

> to be tolerant means: to endure contractions, means:
> to respect a compromise as a solution, means: to
> defend other people's truth against the exclusive claim
> of one's own truth.[12]

Although he despairs at the resurgence of right and left-wing extremism and their resorting to violence as a political weapon, he argues that clandestinity would only increase their appeal. Their power of attraction can only be diminished by confronting them openly. It is this task that the political activist has taken upon himself, so that all his political endeavours are variations on one theme: beware of extremism, right or left, beware of ideologies, beware of dogmas, systems, religions, utopias. Man is self-made, and history is man-made—hence no room for fatalism or predestination of any kind. One wonders if Grass's *credo* is not just as much a utopia as that of his ideology-bound, red-ivory-tower Marxist fellow writers. But Grass himself is convinced he is fighting the 'Hegelian phantom', mainly because his principles, unlike those of his colleagues, actually engender concrete political action.

In 1965, during his first election campaign, the conscious non-party member Grass was still considered an embarrassment by the officials of the SPD. Whereas the Social Democrats tried to wean away the middle classes from the Christian Democrats by appearing as respectable as possible, Grass deliberately upset the balance by emphasising the real differences between the two parties. Not only did he remind the public of the SPD's working-class origins, but he put forward controversial policies—such as demanding the recognition of the Oder-Neisse line—which the SPD would rather have left out during an election.

In 1969, however, Grass's election campaign was not only encouraged, but officially sponsored by the SPD. This *volte-face* is to be attributed to a mutual rapprochement: many policies that seemed treacherous to the SPD in 1965 had become official party policy by 1969; conversely, by abandoning the most radical issues of his political philosophy, Grass could be relied upon to expound the accepted party line. Although he is still not a paid-up party

12. *Die Zeit*, 7 February 1969, p. 3.

member, his identification with the fortunes of the SPD and Willy Brandt is almost complete. The reversal of the SPD's role in 1970 from a party of opposition to one of government has also meant a drastic adjustment for Grass: the protester is now assuming the role of a defender.

Grass's political participation rests solely on his belief in his civic responsibilities, they themselves constitute his commitment. Theories of commitment, whether in politics or literature, he leaves to his misguided fellow-writers, its practice is his. We stressed 'civic' responsibilities, yet we know that despite, or precisely because of, his loud protestations, Grass does *not* do something 'self-evident' (as the title of one of his speeches suggests) when he campaigns for the SPD, that he is both exploiting his fame and feeling self-conscious about his position as a writer. Sometimes he is impelled to bridge the gap between electioneering and being a writer, either by pre-empting possible ridicule by his election audiences or, as in the following passage, establishing a link between the writer's and the politician's trade:

> Who is speaking to you today? A man who has written a record of *Dog Years*, has pumped the stomach of guilt and poked about in ruins and scrap piles for traces of shame.[13]

But when it comes to other people's works, this fusion between politics and literature is recognised much more unequivocally. Anna Seghers was one example, Georg Büchner another:

> (His) prolific but still explosive work played no small part in deciding me to open my mouth, and influenced the style of my campaign speeches,[14]

Grass proclaims in his acceptance lecture for the Georg Büchner Prize.

In his lecture 'On my Master Döblin', Grass makes Döblin the paradigm of the writer/politician. He quotes Döblin's definition of the novel as a manifesto, behind which the author hides, leaving

13. *SO*, p. 11.
14. *SO*. p. 40.

the reader to judge the work independently, irrespective of the author's intentions. But the ideology of that manifesto is that of anti-ideology. Both Grass and Döblin believe in an anti-theoretical, anti-dogmatic approach to artistic creation. A novel is to capture reality in all its 'breathlessness' and versatility, without subjugating it to theories.

Döblin's novel *Wallenstein* exemplifies all the features which Grass admires in his teacher. The fact that Grass should pick on this novel, rather than on Döblin's masterpiece *Berlin Alexanderplatz*, is in itself remarkable. No doubt, the historical subject must have determined his choice, a subject for which Grass himself shows some predisposition, from *The Tin Drum* to his latest novel *From the Diary of a Snail*. Hence Grass's analysis of *Wallenstein* concentrates on the treatment of history as a particular kind of reality.

The beginning of the lecture is confusingly provocative:

> *Wallenstein* [is] not an historical novel. Döblin looks at history as an absurd process.[15]

So does Grass, yet neither of them resigns himself to political inactivity as a logical conclusion to this insight. In their art, identical techniques reflect their common concept of history. When Grass describes how Döblin relegates the most vital historical material to subsidiary clauses, he might as well be talking about his own novels.

Döblin's Wallenstein, in contrast to Schiller's valiant warrior, is above all a ruthless financial genius, who only occasionally fights battles, using the army as a 'capital investment'. Grass shudders at the accuracy of Döblin's retrospective vision, because in his view, Döblin's rendering of the Thirty Years' War is in some measure an anticipation of the economic background of German militarism in both world wars:

> Long before Krupp made *his* big deal at Verdun, Wallenstein invested his capital in armaments. Krupp and Wallenstein each bought a Kaiser. And we still do not want to recognise the fact that it was not Hitler

15. *LD.* p. 8.

who bought industry, but rather industry—disciples
of Wallenstein—who bought its Hitler.[16]

Another political issue that Grass extrapolates from Döblin's
Wallenstein is an explanation for the failure of disarmament
conferences:

> Since Döblin has taught us to consider Wallenstein as
> a master of high finance, we know that disarmament
> conferences do not always fail because of lack of good
> will on the part of the negotiating partners, but often
> enough because of the interests of industry, which
> knows how to represent everybody's interest. Dis-
> armament could lead us into difficulties. The
> Wallenstein system demands standing armies.[17]

Grass concludes his lecture by warmly recommending his
'master Döblin' to the public, once again affirming his belief in
the pedagogical function of literature.

> [I] want to seduce you to Döblin. He will perturb
> your dreams; you will have to swallow hard; you
> won't find him tasty; he is indigestible and doesn't
> agree with you. But he will change the reader. Whoever
> is self-sufficient beware of Döblin.[18]

Grass's Döblin speech demonstrates how an imaginative, anti-
ideological approach to history can represent a comment on
contemporary political issues. Grass's Shakespeare speech with
the deliberately presumptuous title 'The Prehistory and Post-
history of the Tragedy of *Coriolanus* from Livy and Plutarch via
Shakespeare down to Brecht and Myself'[19] also deals with the
transformation of history in literature. It acts foremost as a preface to *The Plebeans Rehearse the Uprising*, thus anticipating an
interpretation of an as yet unwritten play. But quite apart from

16. *LD*. p. 17.
17. *LD*. p. 17.
18. *LD*. p. 26.
19. *P*. pp. vii–xxxvi.

the play, the Shakespeare speech is an essential counterpart to Grass's Döblin speech. If Döblin's *Wallenstein* served as an object of demonstration for all the commendable things in literature, Brecht's *Coriolan* is presented as the incarnation of ill-advised literary practice.

In his address, Grass traces the relationship between Livy's and Plutarch's representations of the political theme of Coriolanus, and its literary appropriation by Shakespeare and Brecht. In fact, he uses Shakespeare's *Coriolanus* as a foil to show up the dramatic deficiencies of Brecht's *Coriolan*. Here, as in Döblin's *Wallenstein*, he deals with the question of history in literature as a 'reflection of current events'. But in contrast to his approbatory attitude to Döblin's novel, he condemns Brecht's Marxist adaptation of Shakespeare's *Coriolanus* on the grounds that it involves a violation of Coriolanus's character:

> No party can claim him for itself by putting a new interpretation on him, because he is not the least bit ambiguous,[20]

by which Grass, paradoxically, means that Coriolanus 'stands between two classes'. This is Grass's reading of Shakespeare. But to Brecht, the self-declared enemy of the people, Coriolanus, is by definition a friend of its oppressors, the Patricians.

The whole line of Grass's argument comes down to the unforgivable reproach that Brecht falsifies Shakespeare. But even if one could accept Grass's view of *Coriolanus*, namely that Shakespeare concentrates exclusively on the psychology of the character and ignores political implications, why, one may well ask, should Brecht be any less entitled to his Marxist interpretation of the play than Shakespeare was to his psychological one?

Grass tries to justify on artistic grounds his criticism of Brecht's *Coriolan* as a failure—his version has deprived the tragedy of its naïve plot and replaced it with a hard-working mechanism. . . .[21] He substantiates his verdict by illustrating how this mechanism is applied to the portrayal of the crowds and the tribunes. In Shakespeare, the plebeians are a despicable and selfish lot, only

20. *P.* p. xiv.
21. *P.* p. xxii.

interested in the betterment of their material condition. In Brecht, they become staunch class-conscious revolutionaries. Shakespeare's tragedy ends with the fall of a hero, Brecht's didactic play ends on a note of triumph for the plebeians. Grass's summary, contrasting the two versions, shows how Brecht manipulated the material to serve his own ideological purpose:

> [His] tribunes behave in accordance with his thesis: while Shakespeare displays two interchangeable zeros, . . . Brecht gradually transfers the power to two shrewd and progressive functionaries. While Shakespeare makes his Coriolanus a man of the highest merit, . . . Brecht reduces his Coriolan to the level of an efficient specialist, who, though useful in time of war, oversteps his functions in peacetime and is therefore dismissed by the people and its elected tribunes.[22]

Grass takes violent exception to such tendentiousness. He accuses Brecht of 'transforming the original, even at the expense of sacrificing the most flowery passages of the dialogue, into a play of partisanship.'[23] For him, Brecht's Marxist adaptation simply exemplifies how 'partisanship flattens out the details and tolerates poetry at most as an incidental ornament'.[24] On the other hand, Grass is full of praise for Brecht's adaptation of Marlowe's *Edward II*:

> Brecht showed us with his *Life of Edward II of England*, how a powerful adaptation can breathe life that has gone flat, how indeed it can give the original back to the stage. He did not succeed in doing the same for *Coriolanus*.[25]

Why defend this early adaptation of an Elizabethan play and rule out a later one? What is common to Döblin's *Wallenstein* and

22. *P*. p. xv.
23. *P*. p. xx.
24. *P*. p. xxi.
25. *P*. p. xxii.

Brecht's *Edward II?* Grass may believe that his condemnation of
Coriolan is based on purely aesthetic criteria, but one suspects that
underlying his aesthetic judgment there lurks a political bias
against Brecht's Marxism. This is also consistent with Grass's
praise of Döblin's markedly non-ideological novel *Wallenstein*.
The literary critic and the political activist get in each other's
way.

Grass himself is convinced that he is incapable of such dereliction, claiming again and again that he can successfully compartmentalise his writing and his political activities. In his famous
Princeton speech 'On Writers as Court Jesters and on Non-existent Courts',[26] the committed writer, for Grass invariably
synonymous with the ideologically committed artist, is held up to
bitter mockery:

> Is a horse whiter because we call it white? And is a
> writer who says he is 'committed' a white horse? We
> are all familiar with the writer who, far removed
> from the poet and the fool, but not satisfied with the
> naked designation of his trade, appends an adjective,
> calling himself and encouraging others to call him a
> 'committed writer'. . . . From the start, before even
> inserting his paper into the typewriter, the committed
> writer writes, not novels, poems or comedies, but
> 'committed literature'. When a literature is thus
> plainly stamped, the obvious implication is that all
> other literature is 'uncommitted'. Everything else,
> which takes in a good deal, is art for art's sake.[27]

But for Grass, art cannot be the result of a conscious attitude.
To him it is characterised by all the unpredictable, sensuous
attributes sneered at by his hypothetical committed writer. His
political activities, on the other hand, are the direct outcome of
sober deliberations. Therefore, according to Grass himself,
literature and politics are completely divorced from one another.
Those writers who want to take part in politics must be prepared

26. *SO.* pp. 47–53.
27. *SO.* pp. 49–50.

to 'bolt from their desks and busy themselves with the trivia of democracy'. Armchair politicians are not for Grass. Notwithstanding the evidence of his own literary practice, the only explicit statement that Grass makes on the subject of politics and literature reads like an irreversible dictum, that the two are forever irreconcilable—'Something we must get through our heads is this: a poem knows no compromise, but men live by compromise.'[28] Nevertheless, the writer has a moral obligation to act. His political activities may seem of no consequence, but, paradoxically, they represent the only opportunity he has of influencing his environment—'The individual who can stand up under this contradiction and act is a fool and will change the world.'[29]

With *The Plebeians Rehearse the Uprising*, the play that dramatises the dilemma of the writer and the political activist, Grass shows in the figure of the Boss, an individual who 'cannot stand up under this contradiction', because he wants to be more than a 'fool' and therefore will not 'change the world'.

The model for his Boss is none other than Bertolt Brecht himself and the political crisis with which he is confronted is the East German Uprising of 17 June 1953. At a superficial level, the play is a polemic against Brecht as a manager of stage revolutions, and a traitor to the real revolution which is taking place before his eyes. At a deeper level, it is a highly complex exploration of the discrepancy between preaching and doing, theory and practice. For when the East German workers invade the Boss's theatre during a rehearsal of *Coriolan* to ask for his support, the Boss seems to be more interested in drawing on their revolutionary potential for his stage production than in lending authority to their political demands.

It would seem that the play allows of two contradictory interpretations. If initially the Boss's non-involvement seems to be reprehensible, retrospectively, his behaviour is, if not justified, at least understandable. Much to Grass's annoyance, critics have on the whole labelled *The Plebeians* (his first full-length play) an anti-Brecht play. Yet Grass himself is largely to be blamed for this misunderstanding, by writing in his Shakespeare speech that the

28. *SO*. p. 53.
29. *SO*. p. 53.

Boss wishes to derive benefit from the current events for his production of *Coriolan*[30]

> The workers try to win him over to their revolt; he
> uses the workers for the staging of his plebeian
> uprising,[31]

or more conclusively still:

> as usual, everything turns to theater in his hands, . . .
> everything for him becomes an aesthetic question: a
> man of the theater, serene and untroubled.[32]

Judging by the Shakespeare speech the solution to the Boss's dilemma is suspiciously simple: had he not been such an egocentric aesthete, had he been the genuine revolutionary he had pledged himself to be, the Boss would have supported the workers without hesitation. What is more, his manifesto might have turned the failure of the uprising into a success, perhaps even kept the Soviet tanks at bay!

One wonders if Grass could seriously subscribe to such a simplified view of politics. Should he really have conceived of the Boss as a maker of history, a saviour *manqué*, guilty of treason because he preaches revolution as a form of art, but does not practice it as a way of life? The truth is that Grass must have changed his mind in the two intervening years between the Shakespeare speech and his play. Although initially his position towards Brecht might have been one of disapproval, the Boss asserted his independence during the writing of the play, a process to which Grass himself refers. The result is an open-ended assessment, one which makes the Boss emotionally guilty, but absolves him intellectually. As one critic puts it: 'He was right and wrong.'[33]

Grass's tentative comments *after* the production of the play stand in sharp contrast to his harsh judgments before the play

30. *P.* p. xxxv.
31. *P.* p. xxxv.
32. *P.* p. xxxvi.
33. Volker Klotz, 'Ein deutsches Trauerspiel' in Loschütz, p. 133.

was written.[34] Defending himself against accusations of having written an anti-Brecht play, he advocates the play as a search towards a 'third way'. Blame is evenly distributed between the Boss *and* the workers, between the West's denial of moral support to the East German workers and the use of force against the uprising by the Soviet Union. One could argue that the Boss in the play also chooses a 'third way'. He hesitates to write the workers' manifesto, but he also rejects with scorn the advances of the government spokesman Kozanka. The play therefore ought to be a eulogy on Brecht rather than a condemnation of him.

But *The Plebeians Rehearse the Uprising* is neither. It is primarily concerned with stating the dilemma in which any intellectual might find himself. The 'German Tragedy' referred to in the sub-title does not only relate to the uprising. This play is in fact the 'tragedy of theory'.[35] In the same way that Heidegger's jargon blinded the youngsters in *Dog Years* to the bones of the Stutthof concentration camp, the Boss's concept of revolutionary art blinds him to the reality of the revolution. It is true that the Boss's arrogance towards the workers seems at first unwarranted. However, this is only one side of the story.

For when the workers fall into the trap of the Menenius fable, they prove the Boss sadly right. By accepting unquestioningly the natural heirarchy of men as proclaimed in Erwin's version of the fable, the East German workers, like their Roman counterparts, have demonstrated that their revolutionary consciousness is not sufficiently developed to stand up to Erwin's brainwashing.

The reversal between the builders and the Boss also applies to the ensemble, and particularly to Volumnia. Though having distanced herself from the Boss during the uprising and identified with the workers, she is, after the defeat, the first to plead for the Boss's signature to Kozanka's manifesto—a signature which is to seal the suppression of the uprising. Volumnia's immediate *volte-face* unmasks as opportunism her previous sympathy for the uprising, whereas the Boss's seeming indecisiveness is revealed as a deeper insight into the political immaturity of the workers. One

34. *Christ und Welt,* 11 November 1966, p. 19.
35. Volker Klotz, *op. cit.* p. 133.

of the paradoxes of the play is that only the collapse of the rebellion can convince the Boss of its necessity.

The play compresses three levels of historical consciousness into one and the same text: the Shakespearian view of the Roman level, the Brechtian adaptation of it and finally Grass's own level. In Grass the Boss and the East German workers vacillate between Shakespeare's and Brecht's version. What Grass says of Coriolanus ('he stands between two classes') is far more applicable to the Boss than it is to Coriolanus. The workers want the Boss as a leader, but the leader ought to come from *their* midst, for the Boss's function is, according to one critic,[36] to stay outside and supply an intellectual foundation; the revolutionary practice should come from the workers. The Boss is guilty both ways, first by not participating and then by participating. His final outcry, 'Bowed down with guilt, I accuse you!'[37] reveals that he is entirely aware of his paradoxical situation. Thus, far from being a simplistic indictment, *The Plebeians* reveals a deep understanding of Brecht's dilemma and concludes that, given his premises, the Boss could not have acted differently.

What the play does query, however, are those premises themselves; if the Boss had never fostered the illusion that political art could be a substitute for politics, conceiving of his art as a form of secondary action, the deadlock could have been avoided. Had he drawn a strict demarcation line between the two activities, the Boss's position would not lay itself open to criticism from both the artistic and the political angle. The artist Grass accuses him of tendentiousness, the political activist denounces him as an aesthete.

But even this is an over-simplification. There is ambivalence, because Grass speaks both as an outsider and an insider to the problem, as one who partakes in it in his writing, and one who presumes to have solved it in his political life. As a practitioner of committed literature, he must, like the Boss, believe in the educational function of art, otherwise this play would not have been written. As a political activist, he cannot but disapprove of the Boss's aloofness. *The Plebeians Rehearse the Uprising* is a literary

36. Heinz Ide, 'Die Geschichte und ihre Dramatiker', *Beihefte zum Jahrbuch der schlesischen Friedrich-Wilhelms-Universität zu Breslau*, Band 7, 1967, pp. 121–43.
37. *P.* p. 111.

equivalent of Grass's polemical Princeton speech. In the latter he claims to have solved the problem by dividing himself into a writer and a political activist. In the play he shows both the desirability of such a categorical division, and its practical impossibility.

6   The Political Activist as Writer

The practical impossibility of maintaining a categorical distinction between writer and political activist is best exemplified by Grass's most recent prose works, *Local Anaesthetic* (1969) and *From the Diary of a Snail* (1972).[1] *The Plebeians* represents a turning point in Grass's literary development. Not only does the play depart from the Danzig milieu and the childhood world of Oskar, Mahlke, Amsel and Matern, it also moves forward historically by dealing with a post-war event set against a three-dimensional time structure. It is also a turning point in that it thematises overtly (and not through drums, Adam's apple, or scarecrows) the tug of war between life and art, politics and literature. *Local Anaesthetic* begins where *The Plebeians* left off.

The figure of the didactic playwright Boss/Brecht has made way for that of the teacher Starusch, an exemplary teacher at that, for he teaches German and 'of course' history. Being primarily a reflective novel, the plot is simply there to illustrate Grass's political preoccupations in the 1960s, which the author steeps in the psychological framework of the generation gap. Young Scherbaum, a seventeen-year-old pupil of Starusch's, is indignant about the Vietnam war and the ease with which his fellow-men take crime in their stride. As a remedy he decides reluctantly to burn his beloved dog in front of the cake-eating women of Berlin's Kurfürstendamm, conceiving of this act as one of demonstrative enlightenment. The burning is to bring home to them 'the horrors of Napalm, as it affects the population of Vietnam.' Starusch's function is firstly to convince Scherbaum by rational arguments drawn from history of the futility of his pro-

1. *Aus dem Tagebuch einer Schnecke*, 1972, has so far not been translated. 'Schnecke' means both snail and slug. To an English reader the idea of a snail denotes protection, whereas Grass implies rather the qualities of a slug: sensibility, vulnerability.

ject, and secondly to direct his protest into what he considers to be more effective channels. He plans his strategy with great care, whilst undergoing prolonged dental treatment. The dentist and a television screen (put at his disposal in the surgery) combine in giving him tactical advice for Scherbaum's conversion from a revolutionary to a reformist.

Like the three previous novels, *Local Anaesthetic* has a tripartite structure, with the first and last part describing Starusch's dental treatment and the middle part concentrating on Scherbaum's plan to burn the dog. Starusch reverts to Oskar's position of first person narrator, but in contrast to him renounces chronology for the sake of condensing past and present—a technique already familiar to us from *The Plebeians*. The artistic principle underlying both this novel and its successor, *From the Diary of a Snail*, is stated in one of Starusch's fictitious dialogues with his pupil: 'Yes, Scherbaum, the simultaneity of multiple activities demands to be described';[2] this technique has far-reaching structural and philosophical implications for both works. Structurally it breaks up the traditional coherence of the narrative as presented by Oskar, Pilenz, Brauksel, Matern and Liebenau; the coherence of Starusch's account is only that warranted by free (sometimes not so free) association and by the stream of consciousness. Thematically, it reflects Grass's insistence on historical awareness. History is not seen as the superseding of one set of events by another, but rather as a constant interaction between past, present and future.

There are links with the previous novels, especially with *The Tin Drum* and *Dog Years*. For one, Starusch is supposed to be Störtebecker, ringleader of the Dusters. There are also points of contact with Oskar; like him, Starusch indulges in irresponsible fantasies of murders and other acts of violence. In Starusch's case, too, the borderline between imagination and reality is sometimes blurred, with the difference that his belief in reason saves Starusch from enacting these excesses. In some ways, he could be described as a contemporary Oskar with an acute sense of responsibility.

Reminiscent of *Dog Years* are the occasional occurrence of Heideggerisms and the reappearance of familiar metaphors: dogs and teeth. Amsel's teeth were knocked out in a fit of rage; in *Local Anaesthetic* teeth figure as objects to be attended to with

2. *LA.* 1970, p. 15.

great care, because 'prevention is better than cure'. The contrast between the uses of this metaphor is in itself symptomatic of the fundamental difference in outlook. Matern's act is an access of senseless violence demonstrating the intrinsic inhumanity of 'radical cures'; *Local Anaesthetic* plays off construction against destruction, it pleads for the bitter-sweet victories of evolutionary cures. The same transformation applies to the dog metaphor: in *Dog Years* there is the senseless killing of Harras, in *Local Anaesthetic* Scherbaum is made to desist from burning his dog.

Much more striking, however, than the parallels with the 'trilogy', are the new features of *Local Anaesthetic*. Most important is the fact that the novel no longer escapes into the petty bourgeois Danzig world of the war years, but attempts to capture the reality of Berlin in the 1960s. Instead of focusing on a single event like 17 June 1953, as in *The Plebeians*, it depicts the political climate of the pre-Willy Brandt days, the student unrest and their disenchantment with parliamentary democracy. In *The Plebeians*, Grass dramatised the paradox of the political writer, by focusing on a committed artist who claims to teach politics in his art, but fails to cope with political reality when confronted with it. The message of the play was that this paradox could only be solved by neatly separating art from politics.

Local Anaesthetic does not even attempt to make this separation, for in contrast to the whole of Grass's work, the problem of art as a factor in shaping political consciousness hardly enters into the discussion. Scherbaum, for instance, dismisses the whole complex of protest through literature as an aesthetic game. Having thus discarded the role of art altogether, the novel concentrates exclusively on 'reality' itself, a reality crying out for change. How change is to be effected is the central theme of *Local Anaesthetic*.

The novel presents two alternatives—Revolution versus Evolution. They are only alternatives in name, for, right from the beginning, the argument is heavily weighted towards the reformist solution. The three revolutionaries in *Local Anaesthetic* are Irmgard Seifert (a colleague of Starusch), Vero Lewand (Scherbaum's girlfriend) and Scherbaum himself. Irmgard Seifert is the most 'dangerous' of the three. A female version of Matern, she is one of those ideologists whom Grass abhors. Twenty years ago she believed in Hitler, now she believes in the socialist revolution. As she is incapable of cool political analysis, her remembrance of the past takes the form of a ritual; she clings to her guilt and obsessively magnifies her failures. Seifert longs for purification and redemption. In Scherbaum she has found her sacrificial victim: he is to be her redeemer.

Vero Lewand's naïve revolutionary fervour and her pseudo-messianic hopes for a new world are akin to Irmgard Seifert's. She too depends on a 'liberating deed', and the most trivial activities go some way to quench her thirst for salvation. Her frequent contacts with her Maoist friends not only give her a feeling of belonging but provide her with a leftist jargon, behind which she hides. Everything she does, says or feels remains on the surface. Whether it concerns politics or sex, her progressiveness is either unthinking provocation or just modishness. Vero Lewand and Irmgard Seifert are both revolutionaries for the wrong reasons: the teacher wants to escape from her past identity, the pupil hopes to forge an identity for herself with the help of the revolutionary movement—in short, they are both using their political adherence to solve their psychological problems.

Compared to Irmgard Seifert's fascism in reverse and Vero's forced modishness, Scherbaum is the only serious advocate of revolution. If he turns to violence, it is as a final resort: not, as in Vero's case, out of sheer sensationalism, but because he is appalled by the political complacency around him. He considers it his moral duty to draw people's attention to the fact that human beings are being burnt at the hands of other human beings, a fact that in his view, can only be brought to people's attention by comparatively drastic measures. This is the reason behind his projected act, an act at least as distasteful to him as it is to his teacher Starusch, not least because he is very fond of his dog.

In fact, the personal aspect complicates the situation. It makes it all the more difficult for Scherbaum to forget his project, as he is afraid of capitulating for the wrong motives. In the end it is impossible to determine whether he abandons his plan for personal or political motives. The fact that Scherbaum's conversion remains unexplained is the most serious fault of the novel. His sudden transformation is only foreshadowed by the episode on the Kurfürstendamm, where the mere anticipation of the deed provokes physical nausea in him. Thus, actual events tend to make us believe that *sentimental* reasons restrain Scherbaum from the burning, although the whole novel sets out to prove that violence makes no sense *politically*. Yet, when it comes to substantiating Scherbaum's change of course from a revolutionary to an evolutionary attitude, the argument is missing.

Admittedly, Starusch never misses an opportunity to open Scherbaum's eyes to the futility of violence as a political weapon. But there is no suggestion that Scherbaum is convinced by his arguments, which mainly consist of historical analogies, where the 'liberating deed' is seen as 'active resignation', an escape mechanism, a retrogressive interruption of a process of development. Yet, Starusch knows more about the lure of violence than he is prepared to admit to his pupil. When left to his own devices, he projects himself on to the television screen as a would-be murderer. It is only in his capacity as a pedagogue that he loathes acts of violence. In his dreams, he not only kills his fiancé out of jealousy, but, just like Scherbaum, he would like to bulldoze the whole of our consumer society. Bulldozers loom large in his imagination, not only because, as a former engineer, he is familiar with the building trade, but because they satisfy his emotional cravings for clearing the ground and starting from scratch.

The sober, responsible pedagogue Starusch, however, knows that terrorism is never a short-cut to progress. Desperately trying to find a link between himself and Scherbaum, he interprets his Störtebecker past as resistance against Hitler, carefully concealing the fact that his brand of anarchism was, unlike Scherbaum's, sheer escapism. He describes himself to his pupils as 'a liberal Marxist who cannot make up his mind'. Like the Boss, he constantly wavers between emotional preference and rational insight. But, in the end, reason always prevails, even though his decision might be the result of long torments of self-doubt, bordering on self-negation, for he secretly envies Scherbaum's youthful idealism.

The dentist, another reformist, has little sympathy for Starusch's flirtations with violence and revolution. His frame of reference is dental medicine. It is not difficult for him to boast of the monumental progress that has taken place in this field. He freely transfers his optimism in the perfectibility of his craft to the workings of history at large, and takes Starusch to task for indulging in his wild fictions:

I will not tolerate incitements to violence, . . . I will
not stand by while the fruits of slow—often ridiculously
slow—progress, and that includes my practice built on
the principles of preventive dental medicine, are
destroyed, just because your fiancée has run out on
you, just because you're a failure, . . . who draws on
insane fictions to show that the whole world is a failure
and justify him in destroying it. I know you. One
look at your tartar tells the story. . . . Here is somebody, . . . who wants the transvaluation of all values.
Here's somebody who wants man to surpass himself.
Who wants to take measurements with an absolute
yardstick. . . .[3]

He concludes his tirade by invoking the virtues of democracy
achieved through 'small but useful improvements',[4] and the
necessity of working 'quietly and conscientiously for human
welfare'.

He pleads for the abolition of all systems; in this domain he
finds some common ground with Starusch, which both choose to
label 'humanitas'. Starusch advocates a 'pedagogical province,
in which there are only students and no teachers',[5] the dentist
expatiates on the virtues of a 'world-wide and socially integrated
Sickcare'.[6] He wants to do away with the distinction between
patient and doctor, because 'all people are sick, have been sick,
get sick and die'.[7] Up till now systems had been geared with
'health as their aim and standard', ruthlessly preventing a man
'from finding the way to his sickness'.[8] To the dentist, enemy of all
absolutist ideas, this policy is tantamount to an attempt at
eliminating human failings. He therefore suggests that illness
rather than health should be taken as a point of departure, thus
removing the obsessive compulsion to health. His complaint is
that the systems governing the world never helped the governed.

3. *LA*. p. 113.
4. *LA*. p. 113.
5. *LA*. p. 86.
6. *LA*. p. 86.
7. *LA*. p. 86.
8. *LA*. p. 86.

But, paradoxically, even his de-systematisation would have to be carried out systematically, which shows the impracticability of the dentist's utopia; in vain he prides himself on his flawless pragmatism.

His dentistry is considered a metaphor of social democracy. Both can only function through pragmatism. But this arch-enemy of global solutions, this technocrat with a humanist education, this self-righteous ideologist of anti-ideology becomes a victim of his self-righteousness. For a long time, his superiority over the ever-doubting Starusch seems beyond question. Yet, it is Starusch who finally wins the day. The dentist's treatment, his carefully built bridge, has to be sawn through and the tooth extracted. Starusch, on the other hand, at times seemingly paralysed by doubt and pain, succeeds in Scherbaum's conversion.

Starusch must admit that the minimising of pain is a form of progress. Local anaesthetic is not only indispensable to medical effectiveness; figuratively, the title of the novel proclaims that sensibility to the pains outside one's control must be numbed if one is to concentrate on those within it. Strength resides in limitation. This is why Scherbaum with his excessive susceptibility has to be numbed too. 'Since the world pains him, we try to give him local anaesthesia',[9] Starusch reflects mournfully. In the terms of the novel, it means that Scherbaum turns his gaze away from Vietnam, and decides to pull his weight within his own restricted sphere of influence, as editor of the school magazine. Scherbaum's course is an exemplary one: he becomes a living synthesis of the present Starusch and his own revolutionary self, an active reformer, passionate only in his moderation, patient, industrious and always self-questioning. The novel ends on a mixed note of hope and pain.

One has fundamental reservations about *Local Anaesthetic*. Its didactic contention, namely that evolution is a more powerful means of changing the world than revolution, remains a statement of faith. The question of progress, the question of man's capability to learn from historical experience, although denied verbally, is answered in the affirmative by Scherbaum's renunciation of his act. This novel which poses as an act of reconciliation between

9. *LA*. p. 231.

the rebellious socialist student movement and the moderate power-orientated SPD has been marred in its object by basic political misconceptions.

One of its most disturbing features is Grass's personalisation of history, a trend already noticeable in *The Plebeians*, although in the play Grass still insists on de-personalising Brecht by calling him the Boss. In *Local Anaesthetic* one of the models is deliberately individualised; for instance: 'Maybe say Schörner after all, if we mean Schörner.'[10] General Krings is explicitly called Schörner, not because Grass wants to give his novel a documentary gloss but for reasons of personalisation. Analogous to this is Grass's tendency to reduce all political crises and views to psychological inadequacies. This applies to Hitler as well as to the characters in the novel. The dentist who is so eager for reforms accuses his patient of indulging in revolutionary bulldozer fantasies because his fiancée has left him in the lurch. Even Scherbaum's burning of the dog is seen in connection with his father's previous war activities—'the father fought fires as an air-raid warden, the son is prepared to sacrifice by fire.'[11] For Seifert and Starusch Scherbaum's project is merely an opportunity for absolving them from their own guilt feelings; it would quench Seifert's thirst for redemption and Starusch could see himself reborn in Scherbaum's activism, if only to impress retrospectively his ex-fiancée.

In spite of the book's political character, political argument remains secondary. Either Grass is questioning the origin of his own political convictions, or he has simply failed in making a rational case for them. Although the argument lacks in rationality and amounts to no more than a *credo*, the composition of the novel is built along strictly rational lines, so that the novel exemplifies two shortcomings, intellectual and aesthetic ones, at their extreme. There is no doubt that *Local Anaesthetic* is a *roman à thèse*, i.e. all artistic considerations have been subordinated to its message. The German critic Reich-Ranicki traces Grass's literary development when he writes about *Local Anaesthetic*:

10. *LA.* p. 198. Ferdinand Schörner (1892–1973) was appointed Field-Marshal just before Hitler's death, on 5 April 1945. He was notorious for his brutal tactics as Commander-in-Chief on the Eastern Front.
11. *LA.* p. 219.

> Whilst Grass did not want to 'messagise' at all in *The Tin Drum* and show everything, everything is message here and nothing is being shown ... always statement instead of representation, ... instead of images, scenes and situations, we are at best presented with facts, theses and information.[12]

It is not the absence of images that should be lamented in *Local Anaesthetic*, but the use that Grass makes of them. They are no longer integrated in the way they were in the 'trilogy', they no longer evolve with the narrative, meaning different things at different stages, but are fixed to one particular line of thought. Ailing teeth equal an ailing democracy, dental treatments stand for the untiring efforts of the SPD to establish a Social Democracy in the German Federal Republic. The stone imagery—trass, pumice, tuff, cement, limestone and clay—crowned by the bull-dozer metaphor, belongs to the world of violence, of revolution. When stone formations are transferred to the field of dentistry, they are subject to evolutionary transformations. Thus Starusch's tartar, as 'calcified hate',[13] as an incrustation of a politically suspect past, can be filed off, in the same way that his chopper bite, a manifestation of inborn brutality, can be remedied. Dental treatment and rectifications of political misdemeanours go hand in hand: Scherbaum, too, finishes up in the dental chair.

The first part of the book, which constitutes nearly half of the novel, is dedicated to the past, as perceived by Starusch in the present; its length merely demonstrates to what extent the Nazi past still affects the thoughts of a contemporary German. The second part is dedicated to the present as lived by the 'innocent' generation. Scherbaum, too, acts out of guilt feelings, although it is not guilt incurred by himself. His concern for Vietnam springs directly from a desire to make good previous German parochialism in political matters and thus represents an exact antithesis to the Starusch part. The third part, Scherbaum's renunciation, is a synthesis, the constructive integration between past and present, global responsibility and total inactivity, revolution and evolution.

If *The Plebeians* was a complex literary equivalent of the

12. *Die Zeit*, 29 August 1969.
13. *LA*. p. 30.

polemical Princeton speech, *Local Anaesthetic*, as criticism combined with a definite alternative, is no more than a literary version of Grass's political speeches.

This last judgment can be applied with even greater justification to Grass's latest book, *From the Diary of a Snail*. It is in fact no longer a matter of speculation, for the prevalence of political reality over political fiction is stated at the very beginning of the book:

> Dear children, today they have elected Gustav
> Heinemann as president. I admit that I wanted to
> start with Doubt straight away, but Gustav Gustav has
> priority.[14]

With *Local Anaesthetic* the emphasis had still been on fiction, albeit political fiction; such pretence is dropped in Grass's latest work, where political reality (Gustav Heinemann) takes precedence over political fiction (Doubt, the main fictitious character in the book).

From the Diary of a Snail recounts Grass's 1969 election campaign, documenting it with facts, figures, portraits of political friends (Brandt, Wehner, Ehmke, Eppler) and adversaries (Strauss, Barzel), writers, students and other election helpers. It takes the form of conversations between a 'renowned writer' and his children, explaining why he left the family for prolonged periods while he was on the stump. No pretext is made that the novel is other than autobiographical, and while Grass is the first to minimise the effect of his activities, he does claim to have won over 'Catholic workers, . . . protesting youths, . . . and old ladies . . . frightened away by Strauss and Kiesinger', because they wanted 'to do something for their grandchildren by voting for Brandt.' The diary is an unashamedly partisan account with warnings of the 'Black Peril' (Strauss and Barzel) and words of commendation for leading SPD personalities. It can hardly come as a surprise that Grass nails his own colours to the mast as a reformist social democrat without qualification, noting with approval that Chancellor Brandt carries round as a souvenir Augst Bebel's pocket watch.[15]

14. *Sn.* p. 7.
15. Augst Bebel (1840–1913) was a founder member and leader of the Social Democratic Workers' Party (1869).

But this is only one aspect of the novel. As one would expect, after Starusch's prevarications, Grass's political approach is not as cut-and-dried as this would imply. Echoing Starusch's television dreams, Grass's condemnation of the antics of the Extra-parliamentary Opposition is not without envy of their revolutionary fervour, although his attitude has hardened since *Local Anaesthetic* towards their misguided idealism. He speaks of their beauty filled with hatred, and the inhumanity of their crusades for 'absolute justice'. 'Don't become too just' he warns his children, 'or one might be afraid of your justice.' He describes them as 'hard total whole pure and razor-sharp', and reproaches them for wanting to improve the world 'without mercy'.

Political prognostications apart, the book reveals more about the person Grass than any of his previous works. It is above all the inside story of a sceptic who sees himself compelled to act, not as he puts it, for altruistic reasons, but for reasons of self-preservation:

> I admit to being sensitive to pain (that in itself is sufficient reason for me to try to prevent political circumstances . . . that could expose me to unbearable pain).[16]

And to his questioning children, he explains:

> No dogma sustains me. I don't know the solution. I give you Doubt.[17]

By nicknaming his main fictitious character 'Doubt' (his real name is Herman Ott), Grass achieves two things: on the one hand, this programmatic name condenses the didactic purpose of the story. On the other, it becomes artistically viable for Grass to reserve his own doubt for the invented character of the book. However, Doubt too, the father explains to his children, 'even if I have to invent him, he did exist. (A story which Ranicki[18] told me as his story.)'[19] This is by no means the only reference to the

16. *Sn*. p. 86.
17. *Sn*. p. 177.
18. Marcel Reich-Ranicki is a leading German literary critic.
19. *Sn*. p. 23.

authenticity of his fiction.[20] What the figure of Doubt ensures is that Grass's partisanship on behalf of the SPD is constantly relativised, sometimes confirmed and always deepened by the ever-questioning Hermann Ott.

Such a neat relegation of roles—absent in *Local Anaesthetic*—between political propaganda and stirrings of conscience, between assertion and doubt, make it possible for Grass to safeguard his intellectual integrity both as writer and political activist. The clear division between reality and fiction

> I wanted to start with Doubt . . . but Gustav . . . has priority . . .

makes their eventual fusion all the more convincing. It creates a dual perspective throughout, in which reflection modifies and engenders action, and in which the problematic nature of political activism and its necessity are not mutually exclusive. The private and the public are so meaningfully interwoven as to transform the private into the public and *vice versa*. Thus Grass uses his own biography to teach a lesson in history to his children, and public events like August's suicide,[21] leave him with a sense of personal failure. In the end, reality and fiction, the public and the private are exposed as arbitrary distinctions.

How an understanding of history is to be conveyed is a central preoccupation here, as it is in Grass's previous works. The quantitative and numerical approach is discarded from the outset. One possibility is allegory, a method applied through the mound of bones in *Dog Years*. The other possibility is that adapted in *The Tin Drum* through the characters of Markus and Fajngold, 'individuals and their private idiosyncrasies'. With Doubt, Grass has found a compromise between allegory and 'idiosyncratic individual', by stressing his exemplary role. Hermann Ott, a teacher in a Jewish school in Danzig, though not a Jew himself, resists the persecution of his pupils and colleagues, until he, too, has to go undercover. He spends some six years in a rotting cellar, where he not only survives, but educates his brutish, yet basically good-natured host, Stomma and his dumb, half-wit daughter Lisbeth. Hermann Ott is perfect in every way; he has only one

20. Cf. *Sn.* pp. 133, 177, 333.
21. August committed suicide at one of Grass's election meetings.

fault. His capacity to doubt, so fully developed in his approach to life, abandons him in matters of love. Here he believes 'absolutely', loves 'totally'.[22]

Two separate time levels are fused in *From the Diary of a Snail*. Firstly, the reality of the 1969 election campaign, with Berlin and Bonn as geographical centres, and a series of conservative strongholds from South to North punctuating the account of the campaign. The Berlin angle encompasses Grass's domestic life with wife and children; the Bonn angle sparks off discussions of election strategies and portraits of his political team.

Secondly, there is the history of the Danzig Jews, starting in 1933. Thereby Grass establishes a causal relationship between his present SPD activities and his experience of Nazi Danzig. It is this strand of narrative which engenders Doubt's tale. Through him, Grass bridges past and present, for it is Doubt who takes Grass to Israel in 1969, where he meets the Jewish survivors whom Hermann Ott taught in 1933.

The interlinking of the two historical levels is always organic, because, in contrast to *Local Anaesthetic*, instead of presenting characters, Grass presents situations in which the present evokes the past, and the past explains the present. This interaction and fluidity of situations is paralleled by the interaction and fluidity of persons. Most persistent of all is the doubling-up of the Doubt/ Grass perspective. This takes the form either of identification or of distancing. He identifies himself when looking to Ott's admirable life for encouragement in his own political pursuits. But when spouting political slogans on his electoral bandwagon, Grass distances himself from his ever-doubting *alter ego* for fear that his activism might be undermined.

Even without Grass, the characters, fictitious and real, are made to interact with each other, as soon as they find themselves in comparable situations. For it is not the authenticity of a character that matters, but the authenticity of his response to a given historical moment. In their individual experiences of despair, Ott evokes Augst's suicide, Augst's death is linked to that of Adorno,[23] until Doubt's victory over his plight—the most

22. *Sn.* p. 76.

23. Theodor Wiesengrund Adorno was a leading Marxist philosopher, who died suddenly in 1969, at the height of the student troubles.

desperate of all—is hailed as a universally valid one '"for there is no such thing as no meaning," Doubt said to himself.'[24]

What links Doubt to Augst and Adorno is their common 'illness'—melancholy; the therapy offered by Doubt is the snail. State of mind and metaphor are the basis and frame of this book. Their close correspondence is best illustrated by the Doubt/Lisbeth tale, after the primary meaning of the snail has been clarified:

> 'And what'ye mean by snail?'

Grass's insatiable children ask.

> 'The snail that's progress.'
> 'And what's progress, then?'
> 'Being a bit quicker than the snail . . .
> . . . and never arriving, children.'[25]

But Hermann Ott's snail does arrive, if only to prove that it might have been better if it had not arrived. After a long period of unreciprocated love-making with Stomma's melancholy and mute daughter, Hermann Ott attempts to awaken his lover's senses by adorning her body with snails. Until one day, an 'indeterminate snail' not only loosens her tongue, but even turns her into a sexual ball of fire. Doubt now has a wife, but Lisbeth has become so normal that she turns away in disgust from the leech-like snail, sponge to her melancholy. 'Lisbeth's illness had been absorbed by the snail' the narrator reports. In a fit of temper she stamps on the snail that has saved her. The snail is cast into the role of the Messiah nailed to the Cross, at which point Grass draws analogies with attempts on his own (Messianic?) life.[26]

Having effected the cure, Doubt now researches into 'The Snail as Remedy'. Whilst looking for academic proof that melancholy can be healed, he falls prey to melancholy himself, until his supernormal wife has him locked up in a mental asylum.

24. *Sn.* p. 229.
25. *Sn.* pp. 9–10.
26. *Sn.* pp. 314–5.

This parable is an inverted plea for the acceptance of melancholy and snail philosophy as productive allies: Lisbeth's liberation (her sexual awakening and the regaining of speech) ends in her liberators' crucifixion (first the killing of the snail, then her harassment of Ott). In other words, Lisbeth's so-called normality results in dehumanisation. The fact that Doubt falls prey to melancholy whilst engaged on scientific proof of 'The Snail as Remedy' is only designed to emphasise the futility, even the misguidedness of his endeavours.

The failure comes as a surprise to the reader, although it should not, for Grass has warned the reader by drawing his attention to one fault in this otherwise exemplary figure of Doubt, namely that his critical faculties leave him in matters of love. This means that Hermann Ott's absolute faith in Lisbeth's cure was doomed from the start. He, too, went wrong in not accepting Lisbeth's melancholy by exorcising it through a snail, instead of welcoming both snail and melancholy as indispensable collaborators.

Melancholy—the term is borrowed from Dürer's etching, *Melencolia I*, a detailed political discussion of which concludes the novel—has for Grass its counterpart in utopia. The snail has its antithesis in the horse used by Grass as a metaphor of Hegel's 'Weltgeist' (world spirit). Hegel himself has his antipode in the pessimist Schopenhauer. Politically the same duality applies here as it does in *Local Anaesthetic*, for 'the classic question now and then is revolution versus evolution.' Blind faith is set against scepticism, the final goal of the disciples of Marx against the short-term goals of the SPD election campaigners. Delineating his position against the political Right, Grass writes in *From the Diary of a Snail*:

> I owe a great deal to Strauss: the insight that he must
> be prevented and the certainty that he and scruples are
> mutually exclusive.[27]

As for the Left, Grass is convinced that his snail will gradually overtake Hegel's horse.[28]

Drawing together politics and philosophy, Grass concludes his interpretation of Dürer's etching:

27. *Sn.* p. 327.
28. *Sn.* p. 55.

While I was writing this book for my own and other people's children, in which progress is measured by a snail's yardstick I was describing at the same time what it is that weighs on the mind: I speak up for melancholy.[29]

29. *Sn.* p. 368.

7   Imagery, Structure and Style

Some critics like to expatiate on the originality of Grass's language as if it were an isolated phenomenon, separate from subject matter, a medium in which words were self-referring signs with no meaning outside themselves. Roland Wiegenstein goes so far as to suggest that

> the modernity of this writer (Grass) ... does not reside in the subject or structure, but in the fact that linguistic vigour alone legitimates his inventions and that he takes no other considerations into account that lie outside the world created by his language.[1]

Wiegenstein is in fact so dazzled by Grass's linguistic acrobatics that he is blind to their deeper implications. Another critic, Albrecht Götze, takes exception to Wiegenstein's approach

> whereby literature is debased to a eunuch with a beautiful voice and thus deprived of its potency.[2]

He argues that

> an analysis of language ... should never isolate literature as art, because by doing so ... it ignores the social character of this medium.[3]

That this interdependence, indeed, almost congruence, between

1. Loschütz, p. 78.
2. Albrecht Götze, *Pression und Deformation. Zehn Thesen zum Roman 'Hundejahre' von Günter Grass*, 1972, p. xxi.
3. *ibid.* p. xxi.

Grass's literary and political oeuvre exists has been the main thesis of this study.

The labels most commonly applied to Grass's early prose style are vitalistic and unrestrained, baroque and effervescent, dynamic, concrete, sensual, tactile and visual. When it comes to his later prose, it is the lack of these attributes that critics lament, so that one reads with reference to *Local Anaesthetic*, for instance, that Grass's style is 'no longer' vitalistic, effervescent, etc. Rarely is a meaningful connection established between loss of vigour on the one hand and intensified ethical content on the other.

By far the most informative linguistic element in Grass's work is its imagery. Informative, because it is here that style, tone and structure combine in communicating Grass's view of the world, including remedies for its ills. By reviewing central images of the prose works and scrutinising their relationship to each other, one gets a clear indication of Grass's development from writer to political activist as writer, from moral to moralising. Through the exact correspondence between use of imagery and content, the images act as the most reliable guidelines, if not barometers, of Grass's ethical consciousness.

All his prose works revolve around one or two central images, which denote reality on the one hand, and a certain response to reality on the other. The very titles of the books reveal where the emphasis lies. In *The Tin Drum* it is the challenge to reality that is emphasised, a challenge through art. Oskar's drumming denounces reality, his art is an art of protest. Reality is symbolised by the Black Witch, so that the drum and the Black Witch are diametrically opposed to each other. But the drumming, however moral in its intention, is merely a signpost to morality, not morality itself; it remains a quest. As it takes into account complexities of man and society, refusing to reduce them to concepts, there is depth to the symbol.

The drum also has a structural significance, for it encompasses all realms of human experience dealt with in the novel: art, love, politics and religion. It functions as an upholder of integrity, exposing in each case the corruptions against which it protests. With his drumming Oskar attacks all dogmas, demanding movement and life, a life that even includes destruction, out of which new life emerges. In *The Tin Drum* this creed is postulated in a passage about a partisan who, like every true artist, 'undermines what he has just set up, because he consistently rejects what he has just created.'[4]

Dialectical thinking constitutes the most striking structural element in Grass's compositions. In *The Tin Drum* it extends to the individual images as well as to their overall pattern. The drum has its dialectical opposite in the Black Witch. Oskar's drumming is an attempt to synthesise the two extremes of morality and amorality, of construction and destruction. This general duality also governs the details of the novel, down to its smallest episodes. The drum itself is made up of contradictions, for it can be put to good and bad purpose, radiate love as well as hatred, even if its primary function is positive. The negative aspects of Oskar's gifts, the purely destructive impulses, are symbolised by his glass-shattering voice. Such polarity between light and dark is followed through in juxtaposing Goethe and Rasputin, Apollo and Dionysus, Jesus and Satan, and is further evoked in the colour symbolism of white and black.

Duality does not remain an abstract intellectual insight, but also engenders concrete situations. One such example is Oskar's relationship—if one can call it a relationship—with Dorothea. It exists on a purely symbolic level, for Dorothea remains an unknown person. In Oskar's mind she represents all the nurses; as the personification of white, she is the innocent, the angelic, the good, and is contrasted with Oskar's 'satanic'[5] nature. His wooing of Dorothea can be seen as a final attempt to take possession of 'higher things', as an endeavour to unite his own instinctive self with her spirituality. Thus his failure to conquer Dorothea becomes a symbolic failure, just as Dorothea's eventual death merely externalises the unattainability of his ideals. After her disappearance, Oskar transfers his spiritual fervour to a ring-finger—possibly Dorothea's—a symbol of his penis and reminder of his impotence at the time of Dorothea's attempted seduction, but also a symbol of marriage and love. His eventual separation from the finger denotes Oskar's insight into his failure to realise his ideals.

4. *TD*. p. 416.
5. *TD*. pp. 506 ff.

If the drum symbol is multi-dimensional and dialectical, it is also a dynamic symbol, with its inherent energy manifesting itself through musical properties. Quite independently of its owner, the drum generates a moral force, not infrequently to the drummer's own embarassment, as in the case of Oskar's betrayal of Jan:

> Oskar redoubled his efforts to destroy the last witness
> to his shameful conduct . . . namely that drum. But
> the drum withstood my assaults; as often as I struck
> it, it struck back accusingly.[6]

It propels both character and plot. Oskar is, as it were, subservient to the drum, defining his identity either in alliance with, or in opposition to it. This means that the emphasis in *The Tin Drum* is on art, in contrast to the play *The Plebeians*, where the emphasis is on the artist. In *The Tin Drum* the artist is less than his art, he is totally subsumed by it. Thus in the final analysis, the symbol of the drum as a fusion of art and protest, grows with the novel as an organic image of creativity against the background of a fragmented universe, inhabited by a disintegrating Oskar.

This disintegration is even more extreme in the subsequent works. In *Cat and Mouse* the black cat takes over from the Black Witch, replacing the frightening fairy-tale symbol with the image of an animal. Grass's works abound with animal metaphors. Either they conjure up a vicious reality, as distinct from the characters, or they become extensions of the persons themselves, as is the case with the eels of Oskar's mother, possibly denoting her inner corruption. In the same way objects are personified—drumsticks, gloves, cartridges, ring-fingers—animals too, come to symbolise human qualities. Mahlke's mouse, for instance, symbolises sensitivity, the otherness of the artist. It is a mark of distinction and isolation, in Mahlke's case it is above all a sign of vulnerability.

In *Cat and Mouse* the connection between reality and man's response to reality differs from that expressed in the title of *The Tin Drum*. Whereas the drum challenges reality, the mouse is its

6. *TD*. p. 252.

victim. The title *Cat and Mouse* anticipates this uneven fight. Yet fundamentally, *The Tin Drum* and the novella exhibit the same structural pattern, namely that of agressor and victim. Through his drumming, and because of his intelligent self-assertion, Oskar manages to survive the fight with the Black Witch albeit as a badly bruised victor. Mahlke, although self-asserting too, but in an unintelligent way, falls a victim to his assailants. Mahlke's mouse becomes a prey to the 'cats', Pilenz and Klohse, and their ideological extension in National Socialism.

With *Dog Years* the pattern is reversed. Although Amsel is historically speaking a victim, he survives the war victoriously, while Matern, although historically speaking the aggressor, emerges from the war as the more damaged of the two. If *Cat and Mouse* still pays lip service in its title to the balance between reality and resistance to it, *Dog Years* does not even attempt to maintain this parity in its title. Here reality has absolute precedence over art. It is a very crude reality at that, not only because a dog is fiercer than a cat, but also because of the pejorative meaning implied in the German title. In chapter five, we traced the development of the dog image from symbol to allegory. Its symbolic quality is already evident when the ancestor dog, Senta, is mentioned. Its appearance is always accompanied by a genealogy phrased in biblical language.

Such parodies, which desecrate the most sacred rituals or phrases of Catholicism by being applied to unholy situations, are prominent in the 'trilogy'. It is Grass's way of denouncing the corrosive influence of Catholicism on politics; Catholicism is consistently presented as a religious corollary of Fascist dogma. Episodes couched in biblical language always convey the opposite of their traditional content. Instead of transmitting a message of salvation, biblical terminology is perverted to glorify the pedigree of evil.

The dog genealogy is an example of a biblical parody being used in a political context. In *Cat and Mouse* cross-references are made between the ethos of the Catholic Church and the so-called ethos of Germanic games and their militaristic spirit (the school). The most extreme perversion of Christian virtues is that lamented by Oskar in his 'interpretation' of the First Epistle to the Corinthians, 'Faith Hope Love':

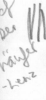

Oskar read and played with the three words as a
juggler plays with bottles; faith healer, Old Faithful,
faithless hope, hope chest, Cape of Good Hope,
hopeless love, Love's Labour's Lost, six love. An entire
credulous nation believed, there's faith for you in
Santa Claus. But Santa Claus was really the gasman.
I believe—such is my faith—that it smells of
walnuts and almonds. But it smelled of gas . . .[7]

Mingling of the religious and the sexual spheres is especially
prominent in *Cat and Mouse* and *Dog Years*, with Mahlke's and
Matern's cult of the Virgin Mary. Even the political sphere is
involved through their hallucination on the battle field. Matern's
sadistic seduction of Inge in the confessional is also permeated
with political connotations, for the dog Pluto 'joins in the game',[8]
with Pluto as the survivor, and hence the living personification of
the Hitler regime.

Existential questions are raised by Oskar's biblical travesties
in the two chapters 'No Wonder' and 'The Imitation of Christ',
in which Oskar puts God's power to the test. Particularly im-
pressive is Oskar's concluding re-appraisal of his life, which is a
remarkably close stylistic imitation of the Apostle's Creed.
Common to Oskar's final confession and to the *credo* is a clipped
syntax, a pregnant word choice, and the respective life reviews of
the thirty-year-old Jesus and Oskar. Both of them are describing
their 'Passion' and the celebration of their thirtieth birthday.
But their paths run in opposite directions: whereas Jesus'
ascension is towards a life without problems, Oskar's dismissal
into the world—also a resuscitation, for he resumes life after
having eschewed it in the mental asylum—is fraught with
problems, which are personified by the Black Witch.

Given Grass's stylistic 'tradition' of biblical parodies, the
presentation of Senta's history foreshadows doom. It runs through
the narrative like a leitmotif. With the description of Harras, this
doom takes on distinctly political overtones: not only does the
dog share the black colour of its symbolic predecessors, the Witch

7. *TD*. p. 198.
8. *DY*. p. 438.

and the cat, but the purity of its pedigree is always stressed: race being an essential part of Nazi ideology.

Harras indicates the turning point from symbol to allegory. When he is first mentioned, he evokes a multitude of coincidences and associations, demonstrating, just like the drum, how Grass's images function as structural centres in the 'trilogy'. Analogous to the drum, the dog draws together the personal, philosophical and political strands of the narrative: Tulla, Heidegger and the NSDAP. The symbol loses its multi-dimensional character when one of Harras's puppies is presented to Hitler. From now on, Prinz is irrevocably tied to politics (Harras was still susceptible to art, as exemplified by Amsel's 'taming' of the dog): he becomes an allegory of National Socialism. By extension, he later comes to represent Communism as well, with ideological thinking as their common denominator. Prinz's survival of the German capitulation simply denotes a survival of Nazi mentality in the post-war period, just as his trip to East Germany is supposed to convey a leftist variety of Fascism practised in the German Democratic Republic. When Prinz, who is now called Pluto, is finally destined to guard the scarecrow hell, he becomes an overall allegory of ideological thinking.

Although art is not mentioned in the title *Dog Years*—this is already an indication of the impotence of art in the face of over-powering reality—the novel is as much a novel about art as *The Tin Drum*. The scarecrows are related to the drum, just as dogs are to the Black Witch. The satire transmitted by the scarecrows reveals an even more severe assessment of the portrayed reality, than the relatively benign criticism through the drumming.

The scarecrows, too, undergo three distinct stages, evolving from symbols of art into allegories of ideology, thus finishing up on the same level as the dog(s). They start off as products of Amsel's imagination. As artistic corollaries to the dogs, their structural function is reminiscent of the dogs, in that they en-compass personal, philosophical and political layers of the novel. Personal, because they are a precise reflection of Amsel's state of mind; philosophical, because they transform Weininger's ideas into visual forms, and political, because Weininger's conceptions play into the hands of National Socialism.

In its first phase, the scarecrow symbol is dialectical: it gives expression to the ideology of the day, yet, at the same time it undermines this ideology by caricature. The second phase corresponds to the Harras phase in the history of the dogs. Amsel relinquishes the mystical sources from which his art springs and proceeds to a frontal attack on the regime: Prussian gods are replaced by scarecrow representations of SA men, Amsel's art has turned into an overt challenge to the National Socialist regime. The response to this challenge is well-known; it results in Matern's brutal assault on the artist. By the third stage, the ballet, the scarecrows have assumed an allegorical character. From then on they function as abstractions of ideology, thus paralleling the evolution of the dog image. Like the dog, they detach themselves from their owner, and even reappear in East Germany. They provoke pseudo-scholastic discourses such as the following:

> If man was created in God's image and the scarecrow in the image of man, is the scarecrow not the image and likeness of God?[9]

Finally, in the scarecrow hell their meaning is widened to encompass the grotesqueness of man's pursuits at large:

> Is there a hell? Or is hell already on earth?[10]

Drum versus Black Witch, mouse versus cat, scarecrows versus dogs—herein lies the thematic balance or imbalance, as effected by the images. Their structural relevance is concentrated on three particular properties. Firstly, their *multi-dimensional* character, for each individual image emerges as a nodal thematic point. Secondly, their *dynamic* character, warranted both by the images' inherent mutual antagonism—the drum fights the Black Witch, the mouse the cat and the scarecrows the dogs—and by their relationship to the characters to which they are attributed. Drum, mouse and scarecrows all assert their independence. They propel Oskar, Mahlke and Amsel, but they also propel the plot; they are autonomous driving forces. Far from being extensions of the characters, the characters are subservient to them, as they are

9. *DY.* p. 600.
10. *DY.* p. 600.

indeed to the opposing forces, namely the Black Witch, the cat and the dogs. This *dialectical* tension is the third property; it is essential to the 'trilogy' as the tension between persecutor and persecuted, between reality and art.

In *Local Anaesthetic* there is a drastic change in Grass's use of imagery. The images themselves are familiar—dogs and teeth in particular—but the use to which they are put distorts them almost beyond recognition. Symptomatic of this change is that the title no longer relates to art, nor to reality, but to man's *reaction* to reality. It proclaims a state of partial numbness as the only viable answer. Figuratively, local anaesthesia is the curtailing of man's sensibilities, in order to maximise the effectiveness of that part of man's consciousness which is not suspended. 'And all my pain?' Starusch asks, to which the dentist replies: 'Local anaesthesia.'[11] In political terms, it means concentrating actively on a small area of reality, rather than paying lip-service to the redemption of the world at large; it implies accepting compromise and denouncing the violence of global solutions. Negative criticism has turned into positive criticism. Matern of *Dog Years* poisons Harras. He deludes himself that, by this act, he can eliminate evil. Scherbaum, on the other hand, saves his dog. He is prepared to deal with reality and so does not burn the animal.

In *Local Anaesthetic* it is no longer a question of art versus reality, the title defines the only political attitude acceptable to the author. The imagery fits the message: teeth and stones are purely functional. All the images relating to dentistry or dental treatment—like anaesthesia, the filing of teeth or building of bridges—stand for reformism and evolution. They are keys to an attitude where even imperfect dentures (read societies) are considered an acceptable point of departure for piecemeal improvements. The stone imagery, on the other hand, represents a threat to this reformist mentality. Concrete, and other images from the building trade, notably the bulldozer, stand for absolutist theories, legitimating violence and terrorism in the name of a classless society, of revolution, of the perfection of man. When stone and dental images merge as in 'so today we shall attack your tartar, your Enemy Number one',[12] the inference is quite clear: Starusch's

11. *LA*. p. 10.
12. *LA*. p. 9.

tartar, called elsewhere 'incrustations of hatred', resulting from a violent political past, is to be gently removed by the dentist's evolutionary appliances. The same message is conveyed by Starusch's chopper bite, sign of brutality, which is to be 'attenuated' with 'the help of a corrective bridge'.[13] When the author makes the dentist say 'there's quite a bit of work to be done' with reference to Starusch's dental situation, the political *double-entendre* can hardly be overlooked. If one looks at the images in isolation, they seem to bear no relevance to the themes of the novel; only their relationship towards the main characters and their contrived arrangement make them reinforce the message of the whole.

Although the overall composition of *Local Anaesthetic* is still dialectical, as was that of the three previous novels, the individual images are not. Thesis and antithesis are no longer contained within one and the same image, as was the case with drum and scarecrow; instead, thesis and antithesis are individualised in separate complexes of images. Mere products of the mind, they are equations, lacking the dynamic quality of earlier symbols. As their function is intellectually pre-determined, they are static cyphers, neither evolving with, nor propelling characters and plot.

The change from the dialectical to the linear, from the dynamic to the static, the organic to the functional, the multi-dimensional to the one-dimensional should be recognised as paralleling Grass's literary development from moral to moralising: it is in that sense that the imagery acts as a barometer of the author's ethical consciousness. The more insistent the moral urgency, the less scope for the imagination. Grass's more sober style is not just a faded version of his previous bravura, it is different in kind, corresponding to a more sober view of the world, in which imagination is being increasingly filtered through reason. The playfulness of *The Tin Drum* has made way for elucidated concepts in *Local Anaesthetic*. It is debatable whether this higher degree of abstraction in the name of didacticism does in fact represent an elucidation or whether it is simply the reduction of a complex reality to abstract ideas. Judging by *Local Anaesthetic*, Grass's increasing political commitment has undoubtedly been to the detriment of Grass the writer.

13. *LA*. p. 6.

That this correlation is not an inevitable one has been evidenced by the latest work to date, *From the Diary of a Snail*, Grass's most didactic work so far. The progression from hunchbacked artist (*The Tin Drum*) to artist (*Plebeians*) to teacher (*Local Anaesthetic*) to father, more and more highlights the educator in the writer Grass. The emblem of the snail, as the successor to local anaesthetic is also marginally more tendentious. Whereas the former indicates man's *response* to his environment, i.e. an attitude of mind, the snail heralds the political solution itself. It provides the political answer and indeed the political programme to deal with the devastation left by *Dog Years*.

And yet, in spite of so much rationality, *From the Diary of a Snail* is an exceptionally happy marriage between politics and literature: a state of affairs all the more remarkable in the context of Günter Grass who in his Princeton speech of 1966 had declared the necessity of a categorical distinction between writer and political activist. This profession of creed, which even then belied his literary practice, has mellowed. Asked, in the book, by younger German writers 'whether his commitment was not detrimental to his writing,' Grass mocks at them, because their question suggests to him that they 'were guarding their own talents as if they had to be protected from the draft.'[14]

Far from corroborating his Princeton message, Grass not only acknowledges, but even welcomes the inter-action between his life as writer and political activist. He appeases his apprehensive questioners by taking two beer mats, one standing for literature, one for politics, and proceeds to illustrate his position:

> I created a distance between the two beer mats,
> brought them close together, propped them up
> against each other, covered the first with the second
> (and then the second with the first), and said: It's
> sometimes difficult, but it is possible. You shouldn't
> worry so much.[15]

14. *Sn.* p. 338.
15. *Sn.* p. 338.

8   Grass and his Critics

If I were assembling an orchestra of authors, I might
put Henry James at violin, D. H. Lawrence at trumpet,
Tolstoi at French horn, Scott Fitzgerald at saxophone,
Saul Bellow at oboe, Norman Mailer at cymbals,
J. D. Salinger at flute, and Günter Grass—Günter
Grass would be my conductor. He would lead with
the showy nervous energy of a Bernstein who knows
all the parts, forwards and backwards, can play them
fast or slow, *fortissimo* or *pianissimo*, and in a pinch—
to keep the audience riveted—will flip over on his
hands and lead with his feet. For the talent of Günter
Grass is so prodigious that his only problem is learning
how to ration it. . . .[1]

This exalted eulogy came from America at a time when
Grass's star on the German literary horizon was already fading,
but his political fame was reaching infinite proportions. Whether
Grass's enthusiastic acclaim abroad, particularly in the United
States, is just another example of 'no man being a prophet in his
own country', or whether it is, at least in part, based on a misunderstanding of his work, is difficult to determine. There is at
least one example which would suggest the latter.

The unanimous rejection of *Local Anaesthetic* in Germany and
its acclamation in the United States marked the most extreme
discrepancy in Grass's critical reception. In 1970, *Time* magazine
featured 'Germany's Günter Grass' on its cover as the 'novelist
between the generations. A man who can speak to the Young.' To
a German connoisseur of Grass this subtitle reads like an insult,
for no other of his works has brought Grass's total alienation from

1. Richard Kluger, 'Tumultuous Indictment of Man', *Harper*, June 1965,
pp. 110–2, quoted from W. J. Schwarz, *Der Erzähler Günter Grass*, p. 99.

'the young' so blatantly to light as *Local Anaesthetic*. Undisturbed by this fact, the anonymous author of the *Time* article pursues his equation:

> Like the young of Germany, Grass deplores materialism and hates the repressive power of the Soviet Union. Like them, he is enraged by U.S. support of a bad government in Greece . . . ,[2]

and concludes from this evidence:

> If anyone can or could speak to the Scherbaums of today, Grass can.[3]

But one of those 'Scherbaums', Rudi Dutschke, ex-leader of the militant Extra-Parliamentary Opposition made it quite clear that Grass was the last person 'who could speak to them'; worse still, Dutschke presented Grass to his fellow students (in the 1969 election campaign) as their 'worst enemy, who had to be fought at all costs'.

Comparable assessments in England, such as Neal Anderson's are more perceptive and accurate, as the title 'The Lonely German' indicates:

> Instead of the humane pragmatism Grass wanted, a reborn Marxist ideology of revolution spread across young West Germany from Berlin. Grass's early sympathy with the students in their struggle against authoritarian universities and brutal police turned gradually to suspicion, then to hostility. Always mistrustful of organised ideas, Grass reacted truculently and his less attractive traits emerged.[4]

What these appreciations show—apart from notable discrepancies between Grass's reputation at home and abroad—is that public reaction to his work is always made up of a curious mixture

2. *Time*, 13 April 1970, p. 57.
3. *Ibid.* p. 57.
4. *The Observer*, 26 July 1970.

of literary and political criteria, or in the words of the German critic Grathoff,[5] public opinion has responded to Grass's works as if they were political events.

The controversy started with *The Tin Drum*: an independent jury of literary critics bestowed on the novel the Bremen Award for Literature. The Senate of the City of Bremen, however, annulled the jury's decision; whilst explicitly acknowledging the artistic merits of this work, it withheld the award on political grounds.[6] The publication of *Cat and Mouse* produced a similar situation. The novella was in grave danger of being banned by the state government of Hessen on account of its 'pornographic' content. Fortunately, Grass's publishers were able to mobilise sufficient support among the most respected critics and psychologists to prevent this happening.

In 1965, the time of Grass's first public election performances, the process was suddenly reversed. If up till then, Grass's literary output had been subject to political harassment, after 1965 Grass's literary statements were used to undermine his political pronouncements.

The most striking example of literary defamation being used as a political weapon was in the court proceedings *Grass versus Ziesel*.[7] The right-wing CSU sympathiser Ziesel reacted against a political remark made by the SPD campaigner Grass by describing Grass as an 'author of the worst pornographic obscenities and defamations against the Catholic Church.' Grass sued Ziesel for libel, but lost the case, so that Ziesel was henceforth free to call Grass a 'pornographer' so long as he restricted his designation to a literary context. To Grathoff and many others:

> The judgment is a monstrosity: for Grass's fiction
> bears from now on the official stamp of 'pornography'
> or more precisely 'pornographic obscenities'.[8]

Whilst condemning such extrinsic political consequences of the publication of Grass's writing, Grathoff at the same time

5. D. Grathoff, 'Schnittpunkte von Literatur und Politik', *Basis I*, 1970, p. 134.
6. See 'In Sachen Bremer Literaturpreis', *GD*. pp. 263–83.
7. *Kunst oder Pornographie. Der Prozess Grass gegen Ziesel.*, 1969.
8. Grathoff, *op. cit.*, p. 145.

E

regrets that when it comes to analysing the works themselves, critics have shown an obsessive preoccupation with the purely formal aspects of Grass's works. Grathoff finds it surprising, not only

> because Grass has shown an extraordinary direct
> political commitment, but above all because he
> constantly discusses the possibilities of the writer
> committing himself politically, both in his literary work
> and his theoretical writings and enquires above all
> into the effect of a *littérature engagée* on society.[9]

He laments that

> Very often people can do little else with the
> contemporary Grass than pigeon-hole him under
> the same categories as Grimmelshausen, Goethe or
> Grillparzer.[10]

One could extend the list: Jean Paul, Rabelais, Sterne and Melville are other writers with whom critics have tried to link *The Tin Drum*.

The one common denominator that has characterised the immediate critical response (in Germany) to *The Tin Drum* is admiration for the originality and the sheer power of the work, to which critics have paid tribute with hyperbole like 'boisterous talent' and 'torrential force'. Divisions of opinion did not arise over the quality of the work, but its interpretation. It is here that three schools of thought have emerged: those who saw in Oskar the personification of immorality; those who exempted him from moral criteria altogether, and finally those who considered Oskar's drumming a moral activity.

Günter Blöcker[11] was the most violent in his condemnation of the work as a monument of 'immorality'. He foreshadowed Ziesel's reaction by accusing Grass of wallowing in the worst improprieties for their own sake, and reproved the novel for its

9. *Ibid.*, p. 135.
10. *Ibid.*, p. 142.
11. G. Blöcker, 'Rückkehr zur Nabelschnur' in Loschütz, p. 21.

'perversion', its 'anti-human climate'; he was shocked and disgusted by its 'blasphemous' and 'pornographic' content. Peter Hornung rivalled Blöcker in his indignation. He concluded his review:

> *The Tin Drum* has been called a rebellion. I can only agree with this, but in quite a different sense: it is a rebellion of stupidity ... which ends in clinical phantasmagoria.[12]

Philip Toynbee, although less agressive, would probably have subscribed to Hornung's verdict. To him the novel was not only 'inhuman', but one of the 'most boring he had ever had to read'.[13]

Some American assessments were not dissimilar, such as this one by Hugh McGovern:

> Here is one long, crazy, unalleviated nightmare, void of any beauty or sanity. If you can stick with it and stomach it, you will, perhaps, find a brilliant artistic experience. . . . It is hard reading and even more difficult comprehending. . . . It groans with obscure symbolisms, is rotten with perverted eroticisms, and is revolting in its numerous blasphemies of the Catholic Church.[14]

Or this one:

> When this sprawling, bad-mannered novel first appeared in Germany ... Grass instantly became the hero and spokesman for West Germany's dissident ... intellectuals. . . .[15]

Yet it is not only the fascination of 'evil' that held their attention. Both critics could see some 'point' to the novel. To McGovern

12. P. Hornung in Loschütz, p. 25.
13. Philip Toynbee, *The Observer*, 30 September 1962.
14. Hugh McGovern in H. K. Domandi, *Library of Literary Criticism*, p. 275.
15. F. V. Grunfeld, *The Reporter*, 14 March 1963, p. 54, quoted in Domandi, p. 275.

> there emerges from *The Tin Drum* an authentic feeling, a burning horror and rage at the loathsomeness of the human condition,[16]

and Grunfeld wondered whether Grass

> accuses (his readers) of being midgets or whether his message is that only dwarfs and children can survive the evils of this world.[17]

One of the first and most enthusiastic responses in Germany came from Hans Magnus Enzensberger in 1959. He hailed Grass as 'a peace-breaker', a 'wild loner in our domesticated literature'. To him Oskar's story is beyond the boundaries of good and evil—it is essentially amoral:

> This author does not attack anything, does not prove anything . . . he has no other intention but to tell his story with the greatest possible precision.[18]

Reich-Ranicki argued in a similar vein:

> Grass does not want to convince, but provoke, not convert, but wake up. . . .[19]

But he went a step further. Although he also discarded criteria of morality with reference to Oskar, he distinguished between the actual novel and the impetus behind the novel. Its 'anti-humane climate' and its 'cruel amorality' were far from gratuitous to him; he credits its author with a moral purpose in trying to come to terms with this particular period of history, and praised him for his first successful depiction of Jews in German fiction after 1945. The majority of English critics settled for the 'amoral', the apolitical interpretation. R. C. Andrews for example:

16. McGovern, *op. cit.*

17. Grunfeld, *op. cit.*

18. H. M. Enzensberger, 'Wilhelm Meister auf Blech getrommelt', in Loschütz, p. 10.

19. M. Reich-Ranicki, 'Unser grimmiger Idylliker', *Deutsche Literatur in Ost und West*, p. 219.

Many will find fault with its deliberate amoralism, its refusal to deal responsibly with social and political problems, its coquetries with the sanctities of life and its holding up of the distorting mirror to the whole of humanity. . . .[20]

R. C. Andrews does not find fault with it, nor does the reviewer of the *Times Literary Supplement*, under the title of 'Drum of Neutrality:

Oskar's drumming . . . becomes like a primitive and magical equivalent for artistic creation. Oskar uses it both to recapitulate and invoke past events, and to control or influence present ones—as when he breaks up a Nazi meeting with his drumming. In this way we come to accept it as part of this peculiar story-teller's equipment, no more odd than the epic poet's use of metre.[21]

To Idris Parry,[22] John Mander,[23] and Alexander Gelley[24] the drum is above all a symbol of creative energy and vitality, a symbol of art and memory. At the time of publication, only a minority recognised the moralist in the author of *The Tin Drum*. Retrospectively, especially since Grass's political involvement, 'moral' interpretations of his first novel are gaining more and more ground. But even in 1960, there were some critics who saw in Oskar a Christ-like figure, as did Karl Migner in his article: 'The Drummed Protest against our World',[25] or those who interpreted him as a secular Messiah. Theodor Wieser, for instance,

20. R. C. Andrews, *Modern Languages*, March 1964, p. 31, quoted in Domandi, pp. 275–6.

21. *Times Literary Supplement*, 5 October 1962, p. 776.

22. Idris Parry, 'Aspects of Günter Grass's Narrative Technique', *Forum for Modern Language Studies*, vol. 3, No. 2, 1967, pp. 99–114.

23. John Mander, 'Variations on a Tin Drum', *Encounter* No. 110, 1962, pp. 77–8.

24. Alexander Gelley, 'Art and Reality in *Die Blechtrommel*', *Forum for Modern Language Studies*, No. 2, 1967, pp. 115–25.

25. Karl Migner, 'Der getrommelte Protest gegen unsere Welt', *Welt und Wort*, vol. 15, 1960, pp. 205–7.

discerns in Grass a moralist, someone who is willing and capable of finding his way out of the political maze of the last decades:

> Already his German-Polish heritage endows him with the necessary distance. But even more significant than his moral awareness is the human insight that no single case can simply be reduced to a legal verdict. . . .[26]

Figures in the novel like Meyn, Markus, Fajngold or Lankes ensure that Grass's social criticism never degenerates into meaningless theory. Michael Hamburger's assessment of *The Tin Drum* as a political allegory is somewhat more tentative; but he still is aware of its moral significance.

> Oskar's apolitical and amoral nature cannot be wholly dissociated from the political events covered by the novel; and though the strength of Herr Grass owes much to his avoidance of the conventional question of moral guilt—the falling of the tension in the post-war episodes does suggest that Herr Grass may have been seriously bothered by these implications.[27]

Finally, there are those critics who arrived at a moral interpretation of Oskar by linking him to the picaresque tradition. Wilfried van der Will[28] is its most fervent proponent: his study tries to show that the figure of the *picaro* in contemporary literature

> represents the indestructible individual, who in spite of his numerous role-changes still manages to preserve his individuality in the face of a corrupt society . . . . The picaresque loner becomes at the same time the guardian of all that is humane. . . .[29]

Mutatis mutandis, the controversy that surrounded *The Tin Drum* and the debate it sparked off was repeated in slow motion

26. Theodor Wieser, 'Fabulierer und Moralist', *Merkur*, **13**, 1959, pp. 1188–91.

27. Michael Hamburger, *From Prophecy to Exorcism*, London, 1965, p. 153.

28. Wilfried van der Will, *Pikaro heute*, 1967.

29. In *Germanistik*, 9.J., H.3, July 1968, p. 652.

on the publication of the two subsequent works of the 'trilogy', *Cat and Mouse* and *Dog Years*. Those who had already taken exception to *The Tin Drum* were confirmed in their disgust. Conservative critics threw up their hands in horror when reading

> how schoolboys, egged on by a teenage brat, were trying to outdo each other in masturbation competitions, how this teenage crowd was lustfully chewing seagull droppings, and how its hero was constantly committing adultery with the wife of his sergeant-major.

The root of their indignation, however, lay in the desecration of the Knight's cross:

> In no other country has such a medal, awarded for supreme courage, been dragged into the dirt as shamelessly as in this book.[30]

The indignant outcries increased in volume when Ziesel joined the chorus and took up legal action against 'this scandal'.

The other group of critics who had hailed *The Tin Drum*, yet had been taken off balance by its 'volcanic eruption', received *Cat and Mouse* gratefully, for they found that their original criteria were still applicable. To them, it was as though Grass had not only listened, but had acted on their advice. They praised him for having learnt 'how to ration his prodigious talent', paid tribute to the 'balance', the 'controlled writing' of *Cat and Mouse*. Such critics as Karl Korn[31] and Hellmuth Karasek[32] went out of their way to demonstrate that Grass had written a 'classical novella', and substantiated their claim by linking it to the theories of this *genre* first exemplified by the *Decameron*.

As formerly in the case of Oskar, critics tried hard to come to terms with the figure of Mahlke. Karl H. Ruhleder discovers 'A Pattern of Messianic Thought in Günter Grass's *Cat and Mouse*.'[33] To E. Friedrichsmeyer Mahlke's Adam's apple is a

30. *Alte Kameraden*, No. 1, 1962, quoted in *Text und Kritik* 1/1a, p. 94.
31. Karl Korn, 'Epitaph für Mahlke', in Loschütz, pp. 28–31.
32. Helmut Karasek, 'Der Knorpel im Hals', in Loschütz, pp. 27–8.
33 Karl H. Ruhleder, *German Quarterly*, **39**, no. 4, 1966, pp. 599–612.

mythological means. . . . It is the apple of knowledge
that lodged in Adam's throat in his fall to temptation.
. . . The novel explicitly elevates Mahlke to such
dimensions, he is called a Christ and Redeemer
figure. . . . In these dimensions lies the poetic
significance of Mahlke in this novel. Mahlke is the
redeemer that fails, an anti-redeemer. . . .

and he concludes:

Thus Mahlke, as an allegorical figure, is the repudiation
of man's hope for himself, a negation of the belief
that consciousness will be his redemption.[34]

Others, like John Reddick,[35] argued that Mahlke's consciousness elevates him above his fellow men—even if it does not bring
about his redemption—and that his perspicacity makes him
recognise the cruel absurdity of the society he lives in. Others,
on the contrary, can only see Mahlke's blindness as opposed to
Oskar's clearsightedness in the face of the corrupt society that
surrounds him.

Oskar's and Mahlke's paths are diametrically opposed:
the drummer turned his back on his environment,
rejected it by withdrawing into self-willed mutilation.
Mahlke turns towards it, . . . obsessed by an ambition
to achieve its recognition.[36]

The *Times Literary Supplement* reviewer saw the 'moral neutrality'
of *The Tin Drum* also perpetrated in *Cat and Mouse*, with the
qualification, however, that Grass's 'moral neutrality does not
preclude either sympathy or penetration', and found a 'discrepancy between [the] moral neutrality [Grass] professes as an

34. E. Friedrichsmeyer, 'Myth and Obscenity', *Germanic Review*, **40**, No.
3, 1965, pp. 240–50.
35. John Reddick, 'Eine epische Trilogie des Leidens? *Die Blechtrommel,
Katz und Maus, Hundejahre.*', *Text und Kritik*, 1/1a, pp. 38–52.
36. Oly Winkler-Sölm, 'Junge Literatur', *Neue Rundschau*, No **40**, 1962, p.
185.

artist and the moral smugness he sets out to shock'.[37] Reich-Ranicki defends Grass against the charge of ambiguity, and compliments him on the 'concreteness of his social criticism'. To him, Grass's new restraint in *Cat and Mouse* is more than a formal accomplishment: retrospectively, he sees it as symptomatic of Grass's literary development to come, pointing forward to a synthesis between 'artistic discipline' and 'moral responsibility'.[38]

With the publication of *Dog Years* the delicate balance was upset yet again. Disappointment spread. Those who had heralded Grass's new 'artistic maturity' in *Cat and Mouse*, dismissed *Dog Years* as a relapse into infantilism. Walter Jens starts off his review, 'Günter Grass has been faithful to himself: so faithful in fact that his new novel is . . . one long variation and repetition of *The Tin Drum*. . . .' *Dog Years* should have been three hundred pages shorter, but even then 'it would never yield a whole', because 'its episodes are too diffuse, the sequence of scenes too arbitrary.' In short, *Dog Years* was 'the badly composed . . . inordinately abstruse book of a great author who has over-estimated his talent.'[39]

The American Paul West's ecstasy makes an interesting contrast:

> The book is a work of genius, no matter how
> cantankerous wilful, filthy, tedious, brutal, nihilistic,
> long-winded, importunate, self-conscious or Germany-
> obsessed you find it. If execution can be lyrical, then
> *Dog Years* is that. But the hangman is far from affable,
> and, it is worth pointing out, this is the second time
> he has formally executed this body. Never has a
> dunghill been reported with such a consummate sense
> of its pageantry or the violence of racism smacked
> dead with so savage a hand.[40]

Angus Wilson, for whom *The Tin Drum* made Grass seem a 'heaven-sent answer to the wide-spread fears and doubts about

37. *Times Literary Supplement*, 5 October 1962, p. 776.
38. M. Reich-Ranicki, 'Hundejahre', *Literatur der kleinen Schritte*, p. 33.
39. Walter Jens, 'Das Pandämonium des Günter Grass', in Loschütz, p. 85.
40. Paul West, *Nation*, 1965, p. 81, quoted in Domandi, p. 277.

the novel's future', was a little more sceptical after *Dog Years*. His reservations concerned mainly 'Grass's choice of a central symbol'. Whereas Oskar's drumming was rooted in pure fantasy, the scarecrow in *Dog Years* 'hangs in some limbo between reality and fancy.' Instead of Amsel's 'strange power', he wondered whether 'it would not have been better, though more difficult, to have invented a creative artist of vision, but not of fantastic powers. . . .'[41] The type of person Wilson had in mind is Adrian Leverkühn in Thomas Mann's *Doktor Faustus*. Anni Carlsson[42] on the other hand, who compared both novels, considered *Dog Years* a worthy counterpart to Thomas Mann's novel. To her, both are 'great imaginative accounts of history', 'mythical interpretations of an epoch'.

What was a vision of history to Anni Carlsson read like a political tract to Idris Parry. It was the final part of the novel he strongly objected to:

> [Grass] is outraged by what he finds: social injustice, hidden Nazis, . . . murderers living respectable lives. His feelings are admirable—for a politician. For an artist they are disastrous. He sacrifices art to morality.[43]

In Michael Hamburger's view, the 'subordination of picturesque and fairy-tale inventions to a more consistently realistic concern' in *Dog Years*, only enhanced the second novel. He also compared *Dog Years* favourably with *Doktor Faustus*.

> Grass has written by far the . . . most convincing critique of Nazism yet achieved in fiction. He has done so by deliberately de-mythologising, de-heroizing, and . . . de-demonizing that phenomenon, whereas Thomas Mann, who had no direct experience of its every-day drabness, chose to demonize it in *Doktor Faustus* and so paid a paradoxical tribute to its perverse appeal.[44]

41. Angus Wilson, 'Blood-brothers and Scarecrows', *The Observer*, 7 November 1965.

42. Anni Carlsson, 'Der Roman als Anschauungsform der Epoche', *Neue Zürcher Zeitung*, 21 November 1964.

43. Idris Parry, 'The Special Quality of Hell', *Listener*, 3rd February 1966, pp. 173–4.

44. Michael Hamburger, *From Prophecy to Exorcism*, p. 156.

George Steiner is the most enthusiastic of them all:

> In his two major novels Grass has had the nerve, the
> indispensable tactlessness to evoke the past. By force
> of macabre, often obscene wit, he has rubbed the
> noses of his readers in the great filth, in the vomit of
> their time. Like no other writer, he has mocked and
> subverted the bland oblivion, the self-acquittal which
> underlie Germany's material resurgence. Much of
> what is active conscience in the Germany of the Krupp
> and the Munich beer-halls lies in this man's ribald
> keeping.[45]

Apart from academic analyses, like Paul Kurz's[46] or the most
recent one, Albrecht Götze's,[47] such unqualified praise was hard to
find amongst German critics. In contrast to their English colleagues, the German critics condemned *Dog Years* either for its
lack of structure or for the frivolity of its social criticism, which
they adjudged as being 'thin ... without satirical seriousness,
more a contribution to the Party Conferences of the SPD than to
genuine opposition'.[48]

This type of criticism foreshadows the hiatus of Grass's critical
reception. With Grass's open involvement in the SPD election
campaigns and the ensuing production of *The Plebeians Rehearse
the Uprising*, the German press adopted a much harsher tone
towards Grass's *oeuvre*. Their perspective also changed. Notwithstanding the political storms that had been set off by the publica-
tions of the first three novels, the works themselves were discussed
as aesthetic entities, and their political content assessed by literary
standards. This was no longer the case after *The Plebeians Rehearse
the Uprising*, which was reformulated by one critic as 'The Plebeians Rehearse the Compromise' or, the author 'whilst training
for the election campaign has gone to the dogs'.[49] Such stereotype
formulae, originating mainly from left-wing Brecht disciples gave

45. George Steiner, 'A Note on Günter Grass', *Language and Silence*, 1967, p.
140.
46. Paul K. Kurz, 'Hundejahre', *Über Moderne Literatur*, 1967, pp. 158–76.
47. Albrecht Götze, *Pression und Deformation. Zehn Thesen zum Roman 'Hundejahre' von Günter Grass*, 1972.
48. 'Bestseller auf Vorschuss', *Konkret*, September 1963.
49. *Konkret*, 24 February 1969.

a clear indication of the increasingly political approach to Grass's admittedly more and more politicised literary output.

Moderate critics, however, tried to do justice to the play as a play, but rejected it on artistic grounds. Those who did not take exception to the alleged denunciation of Brecht found fault with its political naïvete, or at best, thought the conception of the play brilliant, but its execution rather boring. Its reception by the Anglo-Saxon world was not much kinder; D. J. Enright comments:

> The play is less than gripping and I find it difficult
> to suppose that this is the fault of the translator. . . .
> Never mind the style there is so little matter in the
> play. For the most part it is colorless, two-dimensional,
> non-cohesive, unmemorable.[50]

The production of *Davor* (*Uptight*) followed. Nobody was prepared to give Grass the benefit of the doubt any longer. At best, it was of interest to educationalists or politicians. Editorials took over from literary reviews.

Local Anaesthetic did not reconcile Grass's critics. The focus of interest moved further and further away from his literary achievements. Critics no longer inquired into the political content, but into the political efficacy of these last two works. The 'impotence' of Grass's language confirmed to them that political activism had destroyed the writer. H. L. Arnold's comment, 'The public performances of Grass suggest that he now considers himself a political person "including his literary activities"',[51] was a conviction shared by most. The fact that the publication of both *Davor* and *Local Anaesthetic* took place in an election year encouraged critics to judge them in relation to the election. Reich-Ranicki's dissatisfaction with *Local Anaesthetic* as a misrepresentation, a trivialisation of the protest movement was a standard criticism:

> Thus a very serious political phenomenon of our times
> appears in a rather comical revolt, originating mainly
> in the pains of puberty. [Grass] can now count on
> the applause of all reactionaries.[52]

50. D. H. Enright, *New York Review of Books*, 28 December 1966.

51. H. L. Arnold, 'Grosses Ja und kleines Nein', *Frankfurter Rundschau*, 8 March 1969.

52. M. Reich-Ranicki, 'Eine Müdeheldensosse', *Die Zeit*, 29 August, 1969.

With Horst Krüger's biting pay-off line: 'The question is: Who is really "Locally anaesthetised"?'[53] Grass's fate seemed to be sealed. Writer and political activist seemed to have been equally discredited. One determining factor of this dramatic decline must be seen in the self-perpetuating nature of fame: for with Grass's growing reputation, critics' expectations also increased, expectations which to their mind he did not fulfil. The political thinker was discredited, because the nature of his commitment alienated both right and left. The right persisted in calling him a 'red pornographer', the left decried him as a 'pink traitor', as a violent anti-communist, as someone who had betrayed his radical past, who was no longer questioning the structure of our society, and had joined the establishment instead.

The writer was discredited, because he had abandoned his literary past: what critics had come to regard as Grass's strength, namely the sensuality, the concreteness of his language, was displaced in Grass's later work by discursive argument. The artisan of language had slipped into the role of the analyst. Whereas his first novels proceeded by induction, his later work proceeded by deduction; whereas in the 'trilogy' the metaphors radiated outwards, speaking for themselves, in his later works the same metaphors were subordinated to argument. A 'comeback' seemed impossible.

But to some at least, Grass's latest book, *From the Diary of a Snail*, achieved a miraculous rehabilitation. Rolf Michaelis, for instance, writes:

> So he still does exist, the full-blooded story-teller
> Grass. There he is, emerging from the local anaesthesia
> of his . . . dentist novel, descending from the pulpit of
> the political polemicist, creeping back through a
> fantastic casserole of anecdotal snail philosophy, to the
> beginnings of his murmuring invocations.[54]

The *Times Literary Supplement* reviewer on the other hand could

53. Horst Krüger, 'Kein Geschmack für Ort und Augenblick', *Die Zeit*, 22 August 1969.
54. Rolf Michaelis, 'Das Prinzip Zweifel', *Frankfurter Allgemeine Zeitung*, 2 September 1972.

find no noticeable qualitative difference between Grass's last two prose works:

> Like its predecessor, *Local Anaesthetic* (1969), *From the Diary of a Snail* will probably do its author's reputation as a writer very little good, whatever its political impact.[55]

Dieter E. Zimmer reverses the argument: to him the writer has largely regained his old stature, but as a political thinker he falls short. He praises the vividness of the Danzig story, his talent in drawing precise portraits, his unprecedented honesty in revealing his own personality. But he writes:

> this diary of a snail does not primarily want to be a new Danzig story, not a collection of mini-portraits, nor a sketch of his memoirs, but a kind of political reckoning. And it is just here that it is ... astoundingly disappointing.[56]

It is not Grass's political attitudes he objects to. On the contrary, what he misses is a political analysis that would explain the foundation of Grass's political beliefs.

> But it is impossible for me on the basis of this novel even to guess where Grass situates himself between the Young Socialists and the Schiller[57] of 1969.[58]

Grass's worst failing is to 'mistake a metaphor' (i.e. the snail) for a political philosophy. His persistent avoidance of close political argument might explain his success as a political activist: 'Theoreticians would have a hard time in market places', but, Zimmer argues, 'a book is not a megaphone'.

55. 'Forward with the Gastropodes', *Times Literary Supplement*, 22 December 1972, p. 1549.

56. Dieter E. Zimmer, 'Kriechspur des Günter Grass', *Die Zeit*, 29 September 1972.

57. Professor Karl Schiller, former Finance Minister (on the right wing of the SPD), up to summer 1972 in the SPD government.

58. D. E. Zimmer, *op. cit.*

The aesthetic criteria have been restored, the story-teller partly rehabilitated, but the political enlightener is still found sadly deficient in his fiction. Grass has attempted the hard task 'to unite literature and politics not only in his person, but also in his work.' It is an open question whether he will succeed.

Select Bibliography

Only a selective bibliography both of Grass's own writings and of the secondary literature about him is given here. For more detailed information see the following bibliographies:

GÖRTZ, FRANZ-JOSEF. 'Kommentierte Auswahl-Bibliographie' in *Text und Kritik* 1/1a ed. H. L. Arnold, Munich, 1971, 97–113.
LOSCHÜTZ, G. (ed.) *Von Buch zu Buch. Günter Grass in der Kritik,* Neuwied and Berlin, 1968, 226–36.
SCHWARZ, W. J. *Der Erzähler Günter Grass,* Bern and Munich, 1971, 133–48.

I Grass's Works in German

(a) Novels

Die Blechtrommel, Neuwied and Berlin, 1959.
Die Blechtrommel, Frankfurt am Main, 1960 (paperback edition).
Katz und Maus, Neuwied and Berlin, 1961.
Katz und Maus, Reinbek, 1963 (paperback edition).
Hundejahre, Neuwied and Berlin, 1963.
Hundejahre, Reinbek, 1968 (paperback edition).
Örtlich betäubt, Neuwied and Berlin, 1969.
Örtlich betäubt, Frankfurt am Main, 1972 (paperback edition).
Aus dem Tagebuch einer Schnecke, Neuwied and Berlin, 1972.

(b) Plays

Beritten hin und zurück. Ein Vorspiel auf dem Theater, in *Akzente,* 1958, 399–409.

Noch zehn Minuten bis Buffalo, in *Akzente*, 1959, 5 ff. First performed 1959, Berlin.

Fünf Köche. Ballett, first performed 1959, Aix-les-Bains and Bonn.

Hochwasser. First performed 1957, Frankfurt am Main. (1st version) *Akzente* 2, 1960, 498 ff., (2nd version) Frankfurt am Main, 1963 (paperback edition).

Die bösen Köche, in *Modernes Deutsches Theater* I, ed. Paul Pörtner, Neuwied and Berlin, 1961, 7 ff. First performed 1961, Berlin.

POUM oder die Vergangenheit fliegt mit, in *Der Monat*, June 1965.

Onkel, Onkel. Berlin 1965. Written 1956–7. First performed 1958, Cologne.

Die Plebejer proben den Aufstand. Ein deutsches Trauerspiel. Neuwied and Berlin 1966. First performed 1966, Berlin.

Die Plebejer proben den Aufstand. Ein deutsches Trauerspiel. Frankfurt am Main 1968 (paperback edition).

Davor, in *Theater Heute*, April 1969, 41 ff. First performed 1969, Berlin.

Theaterspiele (containing *Hochwasser; Onkel, Onkel; Noch zehn Minuten bis Buffalo; Die bösen Köche; Die Plebejer proben den Aufstand; Davor*.), Neuwied and Berlin 1970.

(*c*) *Poems*

Die Vorzüge der Windhühner. Berlin 1956.

Gleisdreieck. Darmstadt 1960.

Ausgefragt. Neuwied and Berlin 1967.

Gesammelte Gedichte. Neuwied and Berlin 1971.

(*d*) *Stories and essays on literary subjects*

'Die Ballerina', in *Akzente* 6, 1956, 528 ff.

Die Ballerina, Berlin, 1963.

'Die Linkshänder' in *Neue Deutsche Hefte*, No. 1, 1958–9, 38 ff.

Über meinen Lehrer Döblin und andere Vorträge, Berlin 1968.

'Die Zukunft der Stückeschreiber' in *Theater Heute*, Sonderheft 1969, 14 ff.

'Vom Stillstand im Fortschritt—Variationen zu Albrecht Dürers Kupferstich "Melencolia I"' in *Am Beispiel Dürers*, ed. H. Glaser, Munich 1972, 82–97.

(e) Essays and articles on political subjects

'Und was können Schriftsteller tun?' (open letter to Anna Seghers), in *Die Zeit*, 18 August 1961.

'Wer wird dieses Bändchen kaufen?' in *Die Alternative oder brauchen wir eine neue Regierung?*, ed. Martin Walser, Reinbek 1961, 70 ff.

'Willy Brandt und die Friedensenzyklika', in *Süddeutsche Zeitung*, 11 November 1966.

'Diese neue Regierung. Aber es ist nicht die Zeit für Resignation und Sentimentalität', in *Die Zeit*, 9 December 1966.

'Die melancholische Koalition', in *Der Monat*, January 1967.

'Über die erste Bürgerpflicht', in *Die Zeit*, 13 January 1967.

'Rede von der Gewöhnung' (speech given in Tel Aviv and Jerusalem), in *Frankfurter Allgemeine Zeitung*, 20 March 1967.

Über das Selbstverständliche. Reden, Aufsätze, Offene Briefe, Kommentare, Neuwied and Berlin 1968.

Über das Selbstverständliche, Munich 1969 (paperback edition).

Briefe Über die Grenze. Versuch eines Ost-West-Dialogs (with Pavel Kohout), Hamburg 1968.

Der Fall Axel C. Springer am Beispiel Arnold Zweig, Voltaire Flugschriften 15, Berlin 1968.

'Gewalttätigkeit ist wieder gesellschaftsfähig', in *Der Spiegel*, 6 May 1968.

'Ich bin dabeigewesen', in *Frankfurter Rundschau*, 10 May 1968.

'Wir haben nicht die demokratische Reife', in *Frankfurter Rundschau*, 14 May 1968.

'Mit vierzig Mark begannen wir ein neues Leben', in *Der Spiegel*, No. 25, 1968.

'Die Prager Lektion', in *Die Zeit*, 4 October 1968.

'Gewalt gegen Gedanken', in *Die Zeit*, 11 October 1968.

'Der verleumdete Lästerer. Günter Grass verteidigt sich gegen Kurt Ziesel', in *Publik*, 1 November 1968.

'Völkermord vor allen Augen', in *Die Zeit*, No. 41, 1968.

'Friedenspolitik in Spannungsfeldern', in *Die Zeit*, 22 November 1968.

'Ich bin gegen Radikalkuren', in *twen*, December 1968.

'Über Ja und Nein', in *Die Zeit*, 20 December 1968 (on the

awarding of the Carl-von-Ossietzky Medal, 9 December 1968).

'Die angelesene Revolution', preface to Jens Litten, *Eine verpasste Revolution*, Hamburg 1969.

'Toleranz ist unsere Stärke' (Theodor-Heuss-Preisrede), in *Die Zeit*, 7 February 1969.

'Anlass zur Kieler Woche', *DGB Programmheft*, 24 June 1969.

'Wer hat Angst vor . . .?' in *dafür*, no. 1, 1969.

'Sind zwanzig Jahre genug?' in *dafür*, no. 1, 1969.

'Offener Brief an eine CDU Wählerin' in *dafür*, no. 2, 1969.

'Unser Grundübel ist der Idealismus', in *Der Spiegel*, 11 August 1969.

'Freiheit, ein Wort wie Löffelstiel', in Paul Schallück, *Gegen Gewalt und Unmenschlichkeit*, Cologne 1969 (Schriftenreihe der kölnischen Gesellschaft für christlich jüdische Zusammenarbeit, No. 13).

'Rede von den begrenzten Möglichkeiten', in *Club Voltaire. Jahrbuch für kritische Aufklärung IV*, ed. G. Szczesny, Reinbek 1970, 145 ff.

'Was Erfurt ausserdem bedeutet', in *Vorwärts*, 11 May 1970.

'Schwierigkeiten eines Vaters seinen Kindern Auschwitz zu erklären', in *Der Tagesspiegel*, 27 May 1970.

'Über Erwachsene und Verwachsene. Jungbürgerrede', in *Pen: Prosa Lyrik Essay. Neue Texte deutscher Autoren*, ed. M. Gregor–Dellin, Munich 1970.

'Schriftsteller und Gewerkschaft', in *Einigkeit der Einzelgänger*, ed. Dieter Lattmann, Munich 1971, 25–32.

Günter Grass: Dokumente zur politischen Wirkung, ed. Heinz Ludwig Arnold and Franz Josef Görtz, Munich 1971.

Preface to *Deutsche Parlamentsdebatten III*, ed. Eberhard Jäckel, Frankfurt am Main 1971.

'Deutschland—zwei Staaten—eine Nation?' in *Deutsche über die Deutschen: auch ein deutsches Lesebuch*, ed. H. L. Arnold. Munich 1972, 348 ff.

Contribution by Grass about Willy Brandt in *Gedanken über einen Politiker*, ed. D. Lindlau, Munich 1972.

(f) Interviews with Günter Grass

'Ich will auch der SPD einiges zumuten', in *Der Spiegel*, No. 38 1965.

Martin Morlock: 'Die schmutzigen Finger', in *Der Spiegel*, No. 14 1965.

Jens Hoffmann: 'Ein Staat ist noch kein Vaterland. Die Schriftsteller und der dritte Weg', in *Christ und Welt*, 11 February 1966, 19.

Dieter E. Zimmer: 'Politik interessiert zur Zeit mehr. Ein Interview mit Günter Grass über eine aktuelle Fragensammlung', in *Die Zeit*, 27 October 1967.

Werner Höfer: 'Nicht hinter Utopien herjagen', in *Die Zeit*, 28 June 1968.

Henning Rischbieter: 'Gespräch mit Günter Grass', in *Theater Heute*, 4, 1969.

Ronald Hayman: 'Underneath the table', in *The Times*, 18 July 1970.

Heinz Ludwig Arnold: 'Gespräch mit Günter Grass', in *Text und Kritik* 1–1a, 1971, 1–27.

(Anon.) 'Günter Grass—Ich bin eine Revisionist', in *Konkret*, 10 August 1972, 44.

Antony Terry: 'The bloody Olympics in Munich—a German speaks out', in *The Sunday Times*, 17 September 1972.

II   Grass's Works in English Translation

All references in the text are to the editions marked * in this bibliography.

(a) Novels

The Tin Drum, tr. R. Manheim, London, Secker & Warburg, 1962.

The Tin Drum, tr. R. Manheim, New York, Pantheon Books, 1962.

*The Tin Drum, tr. R. Manheim, Harmondsworth, Penguin Books, 1965.

Cat and Mouse, tr. R. Manheim, London, Secker & Warburg, 1963.

Cat and Mouse, tr. R. Manheim, New York, Harcourt, Brace & World, 1963.

Cat and Mouse, tr. R. Manheim, Harmondsworth, Penguin Books, 1966.

Dog Years, tr. R. Manheim, London, Secker & Warburg, 1965.

Dog Years, tr. R. Manheim, New York, Harcourt, Brace & World, 1965.

Dog Years, tr. R. Manheim, Harmondsworth, Penguin Books, 1969.

Local Anaesthetic, tr. R. Manheim, London, Secker & Warburg, 1968.

Local Anaesthetic, tr. R. Manheim, New York, Harcourt, Brace & World, 1968.

(b) Plays

The Plebeians Rehearse the Uprising, tr. Ralph Manheim, London, Secker & Warburg, and New York, Harcourt, Brace & World 1967

Four Plays (*Flood; Mister, Mister; Only Ten Minutes to Buffalo*; tr. R. Manheim; *The Wicked Cooks*, tr. A. Leslie Willson.), New York, Harcourt, Brace & World, 1967.

Four Plays (*Flood; Onkel, Onkel; Ten Minutes to Buffalo; The Wicked Cooks*), London, Secker & Warburg, 1968.

(c) Poems

Selected Poems, tr. Michael Hamburger and Christopher Middleton, London, Secker & Warburg, 1966.

Selected Poems, tr. M. Hamburger and C. Middleton, New York, Harcourt, Brace & World, 1966.

Poems of Günter Grass, tr. Michael Hamburger and Christopher Middleton with an introduction by Michael Hamburger, Harmondsworth, Penguin Books, 1969.

(d) Essays and articles on political subjects

Speak Out!, tr. R. Manheim, New York, Harcourt, Brace & World, 1968.

Speak Out! Speeches, Open letters, commentaries, tr. R. Manheim, with an introduction by Michael Harrington, London, Secker & Warburg, 1969.

III Studies

(a) In German and French

(ANON.) 'Dingsbums und Espede', in *Der Spiegel* No. 35, 1972, pp. 101 ff.

ARNOLD, HEINZ LUDWIG. 'Die unpädagogische Provinz des Günter Grass', in *Text und Kritik* 1, 1963, pp. 13–5.

——'Zorn Ärger Wut: Anmerkungen zu den politischen Gedichten in *Ausgefragt*', in *Text und Kritik* 1–1a, 1971, pp. 71–3.

BARING, ARNULF. 'Kipphardt, Grass und die SPD', in *Die Zeit*, 25 June 1971.

BATT, KURT. 'Groteske und Parabel', in *Neue Deutsche Literatur*, **12**, No. 7, 1964, pp. 57–66.

BAUMGART, REINHARD. 'Plebejer-Spätlese', in *Neue Rundschau*, May 1966.

BECKER, ROLF. "Mässig mit Malzbonbons', in *Der Spiegel*, No. 33, 1969.

BEHRENDT, JOHANNA E. 'Die Auswegslosigkeit der menschlichen Natur', in *Zeitschrift für deutsche Philologie*, **87**, No. 4, 1968, pp. 546–62.

BLÖCKER, G. 'Rückkehr zur Nabelschnur', in *Frankfurter Allgemeine Zeitung*, 28 November 1959.

——'Im Zeichen des Hundes', in *Frankfurter Allgemeine Zeitung*, September 1963.

CARLSSON, ANNI. 'Der Roman als Anschauungsform der Epoche', in *Neue Zürcher Zeitung*, 21 November 1964.

DESCHNER, KARLHEINZ. 'Runter mit der Glorie von Günter Grass. Kleine Lehrstunde über die grossen Schludrigkeiten eines bekannten Autors', in *Pardon*, No. 11, 1972, pp. 42–4.

DURZAK, MANFRED. 'Abschied von der Kleinbürgerwelt. Der neue Roman von Günter Grass', in *Basis*, No. 1, 1970, pp. 224–37.

——'Plädoyer für eine Rezeptionsästhetik: Anmerkungen zur deutschen und amerikanischen Literaturkritik am Beispiel von Günter Grass' *örtlich betäubt*', in *Akzente*, No. 18, 1971, pp. 487–504.

EMMEL, HILDEGARD. 'Das Selbstgericht: Thomas Mann—Walter Jens und Edzard Schaper—Günter Grass', in *Das Gericht in der deutschen Literatur des 20. Jahrhunderts*, Berlin and Munich, 1963, pp. 92–120.

ENZENSBERGER, HANS MAGNUS. 'Trommelt weiter', in *Frankfurter Hefte*, December 1961, pp. 491 ff.

——'Wilhelm Meister auf Blech getrommelt', in *Einzelheiten*, Frankfurt am Main, 1962, pp. 221–33.

——'Günter Grass' *Hundejahre*', in *Der Spiegel*, 4 September 1963.

FISCHER, HEINZ. 'Sprachliche Tendenzen bei Böll und Grass', in *German Quarterly*, **40**, No. 3, 1967, pp. 372 ff.

FRIED, ERICH. 'Grass Grässlichkeiten oder man kann den Grass wachsen hören' in *Kurbiskern*, **2**, No. 4, 1966, pp. 98 ff.

—— "Ist *Ausgefragt* fragwürdig?' in *Konkret*, July 1967.

——'Protestgedichte gegen Protestgedichte', in *Die Zeit*, 18 August 1967.

FRISCH, MAX. 'Grass als Redner', in *Die Zeit*, 24 September 1965.

——*Tagebuch 1966–1971*, Frankfurt am Main, 1972, pp. 325–55.

GARRETT, THOMAS J. 'Oskars Empfang in England', in *Die Zeit*, 26 October 1962.

GLASER, HERMANN. 'Die *Hundejahre* als politisches Buch', in *Tribüne. Zeitschrift zum Verständnis des Judentums*, **2**, No. 8, pp. 883–6.

GOETZE, ALBRECHT. *Pression nud Deformation. Zehn Thesen zum Roman 'Hundejahre' von Günter Grass*, Cöppingen, 1972.

GRATHOFF, DIRK. 'Schnittpunkte von Literatur und Politik. Günter Grass und die neuere deutsche Grass-Rezeption', in *Basis*, 1970, pp. 134–52.

——'Dichtung versus Politik: Brechts *Coriolan* aus Günter Grassens Sicht', in *Brecht Heute* Vol. 1, Frankfurt am Main, 1971, pp. 168–87.

HARTUNG, RUDOLF. 'Günter Grass: *Hundejahre*', in *Neue Rundschau*, November 1963.

HERBURGER, GÜNTER. 'Uberlebensgross Herr Grass. Porträt eines Kollegen', in *Die Zeit*, No. 23, 1971.

HOFFMAN, GERHARD H. 'Günter Grass und Ostdeutschland', in *Politische Studien*, **20**, No. 183, 1969, pp. 53–9.

HOLTHUSEN, HANS EGON. 'Günter Grass als politischer Autor', in *Der Monat*, No. 216 ,September 1966.

——'Der neue Günter Grass. Deutschland, deine Schnecken', in *Welt des Buches*, No. 196, 24 August 1972.

HORNUNG, PETER. 'Oskar Matzerath—Trommler und Gotteslästerer', in *Deutsche Tagespost*, 23 November 1959.

HORST, KARL A. 'Die Vogelscheuchen des Günter Grass', in *Merkur*, **8**, No. 10, 1963.

IDE, HEINZ. 'Dialektisches Denken im Werk von Günter Grass', in *Studium Generale*, No. 21, 1968.

IGNÉE, WOLFGANG. 'Günter Grass belletristische Diktatur', in *Christ und Welt*, 29 August 1969, pp. 13 ff.

JANHKE, JÜRGEN. 'Günter Grass als Stückeschreiber', in *Text und Kritik*, 1, 1964, pp. 25–7.

JÜRGENS, MARTIN. (Article on *Ausgefragt*) in *Neue Rundschau*, **88**, No. 3, 1967.

KAISER, JOACHIM. 'Der gelassene Grass', in *Süddeutsche Zeitung*, 27 April 1967 (on *Ausgefragt*).

——'Von der Traurigkeit des Besserwissens', in *Süddeutsche Zeitung*, 16–17 August 1969.

——'Oskar's getrommelte Bekenntnisse', in *Süddeutsche Zeitung*, 31 October–1 November 1969.

——'Die Theaterstücke des Günter Grass', in *Text und Kritik*, 1–1a, 1971, pp. 52–66.

KANT, HERMANN. 'Ein Solo in Blech', in *Neue Deutsche Literatur*, May 1960.

KARTHAUS, ULRICH. '*Katz und Maus* von Günter Grass—eine politische Dichtung', in *Deutschunterricht*, No. 1, 1971, pp. 74–85.

KESTING, MARIANNE. 'Günter Grass', in *Panorama des zeitgenössischen Theaters*, Munich 1969, pp. 300–4.

KIELINGER, THOMAS. '*Günter Grass: örtlich betäubt*', in *Neue Deutsche Hefte*, **16**, No. 124, 1969, pp. 144–9.

——'*Günter Grass: Aus dem Tagebuch einer Schnecke*', in *Neue Deutsche Hefte*, **19**, No. 139, 1972, pp. 155–60.

KLOTZ, VOLKER. 'Ein deutsches Trauerspiel', in *Frankfurter Rundschau*, 17 January 1966.

KRÜGER, HORST. 'Das Wappentier der Republik', in *Die Zeit*, 25 April 1969, p. 17.

KURZ, PAUL K. '*Hundejahre*. Beobachtungen zu einem zeitkritischen Roman', in *Über moderne Literatur*, Frankfurt am Main, 1967, pp. 158–76.

LEBEAU, JEAN. 'Individu et société, ou la métamorphose de Günter Grass', in *Revue Germanique*, No. 2 1972, pp. 68–93.

LEONARD, IRÈNE. 'Engagement und Günter Grass', in *Beiträge zu den Fortbildungskursen des Goethe-Instituts*, 1969, pp. 66–78.

LOSCHÜTZ, GERT. (ed.) *Von Buch zu Buch. Günter Grass in der Kritik*, Neuwied and Berlin, 1968.

MAYER, HANS. 'Felix Krull und Oskar Matzerath', in *Süddeutsche Zeitung*, 14 October 1967.

MIGNER, KARL. 'Der getrommelte Protest gegen unsere Welt', in *Welt und Wort*, **15**, 1960, pp. 205–7.

NEVEUX, J. B. 'Günter Grass le Vistulien', in *Etudes Germaniques*, **21**, No. 4, pp. 527–50.

REDDICK, JOHN. 'Eine epische Trilogie des Leidens? *Die Blechtrommel, Katz und Maus, Hundejahre*', in *Text und Kritik*, 1-1a, 1971, pp. 38–51.

REICH-RANICKI, MARCEL. 'Auf gut Glück getrommelt. Spielereien und Schaumschlägereien verderben die Zeitkritik des Günter Grass', in *Die Zeit*, 1 January 1960.

——'Die Geschichte des Ritterkreuzträgers', in *Die Zeit*, 10 November 1961.

——'Günter Grass, unser grimmiger Idylliker', in *Deutsche Literatur in West und Ost*, Munich, 1963, pp. 216–30.

——'Trauerspiel von einem deutschen Trauerspiel', in *Die Zeit*, 21 January 1966.

——'Günter Grass—*Hundejahre*', in *Literatur der kleinen Schritte*, Munich, 1967, pp. 22 ff.

——'Eine Müdeheldensosse', in *Die Zeit*, 29 August 1969.

RÜHMKORF, PETER. *Die Jahre, die ihr kennt*, Reinbek 1972 (pp. 106 ff. on Grass's poetry).

SCHWARZ, W. J. *Der Erzähler Günter Grass*, Bern and Munich, 1st edition 1969; 2nd (enlarged) edition 1971.

TANK, KURT LOTHAR. *Günter Grass*, Berlin 1965.

WAGENBACH, KLAUS. 'Günter Grass', in *Schriftsteller der Gegenwart*, ed. Klaus Nonnenmann, Olten and Freiburg 1963, pp. 118–26.

WIEGENSTEIN, R. H. 'Noch ein Vorschlag, Günter Grass zu verstehen', in *Frankfurter Hefte*, December 1963, pp. 370–3.

WIESER, THEODOR. 'Fabulierer und Moralist', in *Merkur*, **13**, 1959, pp. 1188–91.

——*Günter Grass, Porträt und Poesie*, Neuwied and Berlin, 1968.

VAN DER WILL, WILFRIED. *Pikaro heute. Metamorphosen des Schelms bei Thomas Mann, Döblin, Brecht, Grass*, Stuttgart, 1967.

WINKLER-SÖLM, OLY. 'Junge Literatur', in *Neue Rundschau*, No. 88, 1962, pp. 184–5.

WINTZEN, RENÉ. 'Les intellectuels allemands et la politique. L'écrivain est-il un bouffon?' in *Le Monde*, 28 June 1969.

——'Le nouveau roman de Günter Grass', in *Le Monde*, 6 January 1970.

ZIMMER, DIETER E. 'Kriechspur des Günter Grass', in *Die Zeit*, 29 September 1972.

(b) In English

(ANON) 'Drum of Neutrality', in *Times Literary Supplement*, 5 October 1962, p. 776.

——'*Katz und Maus*', in *Times Literary Supplement*, 5 October 1962.

——'Dogs and the Deflation of Demons', in *Times Literary Supplement*, 27 September 1963.

——'Rome in Berlin', in *Times Literary Supplement*, 28 December 1967.

——(on *Örtlich betäubt*) in *Times Literary Supplement*, 25 September 1969, p. 1077.

——'The Dentist's Chair as an Allegory of Life', in *Time* 13 April 1970, p. 52.

——'Germany's Günter Grass', in *Time*, 13 April 1970 (cover story).

——'Forward with the Gastropods', in *Times Literary Supplement*, 22 December 1972, p. 1549.

ANDREWS, R. C. 'The Tin Drum', in *Modern Languages*, **45**, No. 1, 1964, pp. 28–31.

ASHERSON, NEAL. 'The Lonely German', in *The Observer*, 26 July 1970.

BLOMSTER, W. V. 'The Documentation of a Novel: Otto Weininger and *Hundejahre* by Günter Grass', in *Monatshefte*, No. 61, pp. 122–38.

BROOKS, H. F. and FRAENKEL, C. E. (eds.) (Background and Introduction to) *Katz und Maus*, London, 1971.

——(Background and Introduction to) *Die Plebejer proben den Aufstand*, London, 1971.

BRYDEN, RONALD. 'Germany's tragedy', in *The Observer Review*, 26 July 1970.

CUNLIFFE, W. G. *Günter Grass*. (World Authors Series No. 65), New York 1969.

ENRIGHT, D. J. '*Dog Years*: Günter Grass's Third Novel', in *Conspirators and Poets*, London, 1966, pp. 201–7.

ESSLIN, MARTIN (Introduction to) *Günter Grass: Four Plays*, London, 1968.

FORSTER, LEONARD. 'Günter Grass', in *University of Toronto Quarterly*, October 1969, pp. 1–16.

FRIEDRICHSMEYER, E. M. 'Aspects of myth, parody and obscenity in Grass's *Blechtrommel* and *Katz und Maus*', in *The Germanic Review*, **40**, No. 3, 1965, pp. 240–50.

GELLEY, A. 'Art and Reality in *Die Blechtrommel*', in *Forum for Modern Language Studies*, No. 2, 1967, pp. 115–25.

HAMBURGER, MICHAEL. 'Moralist and Jester: the poetry of Günter Grass', in *Dimension*, 1970, pp. 75–90.

HOBSON, HAROLD. 'Rebel in trouble', in *The Sunday Times*, 26 July 1970.

LEONARD, IRÈNE. 'Banging the drum for Brandt', in *New Society*, 9 November 1972.

——'The Problem of Commitment in the Work of Günter Grass' (M.Phil Thesis, London), 1973.

MANDER, JOHN. 'Germany's voice of democracy', in *The Guardian*, 20 September 1969 (on *Speak Out!*).

PARRY, IDRIS. 'The special quality of Hell', in *The Listener*, 3 February 1966, pp. 173–4.

——'Aspects of Günter Grass's Narrative Technique', in *Forum for Modern Language Studies*, **8**, No. 2, 1967, pp. 99–114.

REDDICK, JOHN. 'The Eccentric Narrative World of Günter Grass', (Ph.D. Thesis, Oxford), 1970.

——'Action and Impotence: Günter Grass's *örtlich betäubt*', in *Modern Language Review*, No. 3, July 1972, pp. 563–78.

RUHLEDER, KARL H. 'A Pattern of Messianic Thought in Günter Grass's *Katz und Maus*', in *German Quarterly*, **39**, No. 4, 1966, pp. 599–612.

SPENDER, STEPHEN. 'Günter Grass', in *The Sunday Telegraph*, 30 September 1962.

STEINER, GEORGE. 'A Note on Günter Grass', in *Language and Silence*, London, 1969, pp. 133 ff.

SUBIOTTO, ARRIGO V. 'Günter Grass', in *Essays on Contemporary German Literature* (*German Men of Letters* IV), London 1966, pp. 215–35.

THOMAS, R. HINTON and VAN DER WILL, W. *The German Novel and the Affluent Society*. Manchester 1968, pp. 68–85.

TOYNBEE, PHILIP. 'A Torch for Brandt', in *The Observer Review*, 7 September 1969 (on *Speak Out!*).

WILLSON, A. LESLIE, 'The Grotesque Everyman in Günter Grass's *Die Blechtrommel*', in *Monatshefte*, **58**, No. 2, 1966, pp. 131–8.

——(ed.) *Dimension*, 1970 (special issue devoted to Günter Grass).

WILSON, ANGUS, 'Blood-brothers and scarecrows', in *The Observer*, 7 November 1965.

WOODS, ANN. 'A Study of *Die Blechtrommel* by Günter Grass' (M.A. Thesis, Liverpool), 1966.

YATES, NORRIS W. *Günter Grass. A critical essay*. Grand Rapids, Michigan, 1967.